DREAMS

In six years, the charity Dreams Come True has fulfilled the wildest dreams of over a thousand seriously ill children, but it all started quite innocently on a windy afternoon in the sleepy Sussex town of Haywards Heath. Margaret Hayles met the mother of a child with cancer, whose greatest wish was to meet jockey Bob Champion, who had won his fight with cancer. For several days, Margaret thought about that child constantly, and decided to help. A telephone call to racehorse trainer Josh Gifford won her Champion's number, and within a few weeks, Stephanie King met her hero at Fontwell Race Course. She has not looked back since.

There have been flights on Concorde, cruises on the QE2, trips to the Montreux Rock Festival, Santa World and Disneyland. Stars like David Bowie, Cliff Richard, Boy George, Russ Abbott, Richard Branson, Ringo Starr, Nigel Mansell, Barry Sheene, Ian Botham, Steve Davies, Frank Bruno, and even Mrs Thatcher have given up their valuable time to meet children. The list seems endless, the charm and enthusiasm of Margaret Hayles impossible to ignore.

Against the backdrop of her own personal tragedies, the smiles and laughter of these very special children, many of whom are terminally ill, and all of whom have been through painful and traumatic treatment in their short lives, make Margaret's work essential.

Eight-year-old Charlene Philips from South Wales, a cystic fibrosis sufferer, was taken for tea at the Waldorf by comedian Lenny Henry, wearing a magnificent dress made especially for her by David and Elizabeth Emmanuel.

It was a day filled with laughter for the child who had spent most of her life in hospital. Charlene died only two months after that meeting, and was buried wearing her dress; her parents will always cherish the memory of Charlene's special day.

But not all the children die, and some survive against all the odds. It is hard to ignore the fact that perhaps Margaret's treats have helped them find the extra strength to win their battle. It is the charity's motto which sums it up, *Numquam Desiste*, which means Never Give Up. The children must never give up fighting for life, and Margaret must never give up working for them.

Now, for the first time, Margaret Hayles's own story is told. It is a story which cannot fail to move even the most hardened reader to tears of sorrow, wonder, admiration and joy.

Dreams Come True

THE STORY OF
MARGARET HAYLES

LISA DAVIDSON

With a foreword by
Cliff Richard

BLOOMSBURY

First published in Great Britain 1988
Copyright © Margaret Hayles 1988
Foreward © Cliff Richard 1988
Bloomsbury Publishing Ltd, 2 Soho Square, London W1V 5DE

British Library Cataloguing in Publication Data

Davidson, Lisa
Dreams come true: the story of Margaret Hayles.
1. Great Britain. Critically ill children.
Charities. Biographies.
I. Title
362.1'9892

ISBN 0–7475–0325–7

Contents

Foreword

I've been involved in **Dreams Come True** since its inception six years ago, and have had the privilege of meeting several children whose lives have been struck down by some appalling disability or illness.

Although I can't pretend to enjoy these encounters, I'm sure I'm the one who comes away the richer. The extraordinary courage and good humour of the children, sometimes in the final stages of terminal illness, has had a profound effect on my own values and the things I take for granted. And that's true, too, for the people who have happened to be around in the dressing-room or wherever, and have 'listened in' on the conversations.

I'm sure, too, that a special treat, like a backstage visit, for a very sick child can give a tremendous boost to the morale of the whole family. Goodness knows, they need every incentive to keep going and stay on top of things.

As for Margaret Hayles, the founder and prime mover in the whole venture, what can we way? She's one of those people whose energy and tireless dedication to the good and happiness of others you can only admire and be grateful for. Personally, I'm proud to be associated with her, and with her desire to simply make 'Dreams Come True'.

Cliff Richard, September 1988

Illustrations

Cover

Front Cover:
Joanne Parker and Care Bear

Back Cover (left to right):
Lucy Lee and Madonna
Amy Wood and Margaret Thatcher
Tyrone Campbell, Theresa Minor and Ringo Starr
James Hall and Christopher Reeve
Louise Balhatchet and David Bowie
Helen Burton and Boy George
Michelle Hawkes and Cliff Richard
Shirley Forward and Phil Collins

Picture Section

1 Sarah Myatt and Richard Branson
2 Lee Hooley and Kim Wilde

3   Michelle Whitham and grey kitten
4   Ryland Dowse and Nigel Mansell
5   Pauline Benn and David Hasslehoff
6   Edward Maughan and toy pig
7   Belinda Catt and Suggs (Madness)
8   Timmy 'Toad' Armstrong and Guard
9   Kelly Bennett, teddy bear and David Essex
10 Adam McQueen and Madness
11 Christopher Johnson and Cilla Black
12 Julie Crawford and Morten Harket (A-Ha)
13 Michael Wilson and the Eurythmics
14 Sean Steel and Sam Fox
15 Corrine Wragg and Jim Davidson
16 Claire Lineham and Philip Schofield
17 Gemma Townend and Santa
18 Paul Sullivan and Harrison Ford
19 Rebecca Twite as bridesmaid with toy rabbit
20 Louise Balhatchet and Paul McCartney
21 Michael Strohm and Roger Daltrey
22 Charlene Philips with David and Elizabeth Emmanuel
23 Robert Canavan and Joe Johnson
24 Karla Penter and Howard Jones
25 Stephen Smith and Steve Davies
26 Amanda Hewitt and Bob Geldof
27 Paul Lowe and dolphins
28 Sheminda Rai and Gary Wilmott
29 Debbie Powell, Holly, and Harvey Smith
30 Peter Osborne (Little Pete) and lamb
31 Kelly Hardman, Orville and Keith Harris

All photographs were taken by Margaret Hayles and
    Simon Callagan.

This book is dedicated to all the children Dreams Come True has ever touched, or will touch in the future. While certain children's dreams have been selected for this book, each and every child has been important, and is not forgotten.

Dreams Come True

1

A Thousand and
One Dreams

Elstree Studios, Borehamwood, Hertfordshire. To the Sullivans from Liverpool, it looks like a building site, rather than the heart of the British film industry. There are trucks everywhere, loading up strange-shaped sets, people in odd costumes walking around, and an air of busyness that is quite overwhelming.

Marie Sullivan cannot believe it is happening to her. One day she was in her house in Aintree in Liverpool, a few hundred yards from the world-famous race-track. And today, here she is with her two sons, Paul and Stephen, in one of the most famous film studios in the world.

The studios are filled with the memories of *James Bond*, the *Carry On* team, and latterly, *Star Wars* and the *Indiana Jones* series of films. Famous faces smile down from framed pictures on the walls: Sean Connery, Alec Guinness, Roger Moore and Kenneth Williams, amongst others, observe the latest film stars coming and going

1

through the hallowed corridors of Elstree. As the Sullivans wait at the main door, their thoughts turn to the strange quirks of life. Two years ago, this day would have been unthinkable.

Paul Sullivan, then aged 14, had returned from Boy Scout camp feeling unwell. His father Bill was very worried about him when he had collected Paul on the Saturday, and by Sunday, the lad was obviously worse. He was exhausted, and very pale. He had a nosebleed, and was covered in bruises. His mother rushed him to casualty at the local hospital, and after an examination, the worried doctors referred them to Alder Hey Children's Hospital. They were to go immediately.

It took only a few tests and a few hours before the specialist could break the shattering news to Marie Sullivan. Her eldest son had leukaemia. The nosebleeds were due to his blood becoming thinner, and therefore unable to clot normally, and the bruising was blood haemorrhaging into his skin. 'I felt as though it was a nightmare, and that someone would wake me up. But I knew it wasn't, and that I had to find Bill at once.' Then they had to break the news to Paul.

Bill Sullivan and Dr Macky, the child oncologist, sat on Paul's bed and told him that he had blood cancer. He was silent, and paler than ever. He simply could not believe it. One day he had been playing football with his friends at Scout camp, and the next he was faced with the prospect of the unimaginable for a teenager ... dying. Paul thought about another Liverpool school child, Elizabeth Supple, who had recently undergone exhaustive and painful radical surgery for bone cancer, and who was now back at school. 'If she can do it, so can I,' thought Paul. 'Is there anything you can do for me, Doctor?' he asked.

'Yes, there is treatment we can give you, but there are no guarantees. Because you're young and strong, though, the chances are good.'

Paul was distraught. But he looked around the ward which would become his home on and off for the next two years, at the other children who had been through what he was about to undergo, and made up his mind to fight. 'Right, let's get on with it,' he said. 'But Dad, you've got to tell Mum and Nan, no tears. I'm going to get well again, and I need their strength, not their pity.'

Paul had no idea what the treatment would be like. The chemotherapy almost broke his spirit. The nausea, the pain, the constant aching in his legs due to muscle cramps and the depression, all contrived to make him feel like giving up. He lost his hair, his skin was sore, and he looked scarcely more than a bag of bones. There were three treatments of this kind, each more gruelling than the one before. There was a spell in Intensive Care, when the Sullivans thought they would lose their son. But through it all, Paul fought on, winning the affection and respect of everyone in the hospital.

The family's support system was strong too. Marie's mother, Marion Warrilow, would bring meals into the ward each day for the family, who never left the ward, while friends took care of the younger son Stephen, aged ten. Neighbours organised a jumble sale in the street, and raised over £1,000 for Cancer Research.

Two years after the initial diagnosis Paul came home for good. He was pale, drawn, and terribly weak. It was an emotional homecoming. Marie and her son wept, and hugged each other. Paul was so relieved to be back in familiar surroundings, and Marie was devastated by his condition. He was as thin as the worst Belsen victim and he was so weak that he could hardly do anything for himself. But Paul was happy to have returned to normality, and Marie was thrilled to finally have him home. 'I never thought I'd be so glad to be anywhere. I'm never going back,' he said.

Several weeks later, the local newspaper carried a story that American film producer Steven Spielberg was seeking a typical Chinese street in Liverpool or Manchester where he could shoot part of his latest movie, *Indiana Jones Three*.

'Wouldn't it be great to meet him when he's up here?' exclaimed Paul. 'And what if I could meet Harrison Ford too?'

It was a wild dream, but it was also a statement that preyed on Marie's mind. One day, while watching breakfast television, Marie saw Margaret Hayles being interviewed about her work, the charity Dreams Come True, which fulfilled the dreams of sick children.

'What a great idea and what an amazing woman to do that for kids like Paul,' thought Marie. 'It would cheer

Paul up no end to meet Spielberg.' She wrote to Margaret, care of the television programme, and asked for help.

Spielberg and his team came and went from the North, and the Sullivans heard nothing more for several months. Then one morning, the phone rang, and it was Margaret Hayles on the line. Marie said later she thought the call was a hoax at first. 'I couldn't believe it, and I was absolutely astounded. Surprised would have been the understatement of the year. It was so long since I'd written, that I'd forgotten about it.'

'I've arranged for Paul to meet Steven Spielberg next week at Elstree. Can you make it?' Margaret asked.

Could they make it! Still unsure that it was not a sick joke Marie was hesitant, but soon started to believe that it was real. Yes, of course they would be there; wild horses would not keep them away.

It was bright and early on Saturday 23 July when Marie, Paul and Stephen Sullivan left Liverpool's Lime Street Station for London. It was a huge adventure for the family that had rarely left their home town, and who at times had felt a day like this could never dawn. From Watford, they took a taxi to Elstree, and then the surprises really began. The security guard claimed to know nothing of the Sullivans, or of Margaret Hayles, and Marie was despondent. What if it had all been a hoax? The boys would be so disappointed. A quick telephone call to the press office soon sorted out the problem, and minutes later Rebecca West appeared, and whisked the family off to her office. Sue D'Arcy, the head publicist, was waiting to greet them. 'This is Paul's day,' she said. 'We want to make sure he has a day to remember always.'

Videotapes of *Raiders of the Lost Ark* and *Indiana Jones and the Temple of Doom*, signed by Steven Spielberg and Harrison Ford, signed photos, production T-shirts and baseball caps made up the booty.

A few minutes later, in breezed Margaret Hayles, a bubbly and lively lady in her mid-forties. An air of blustering good humour surrounded her as she greeted the Sullivans. 'You must be Paul,' she said, giving him a hug. 'I hope you're enjoying yourself. This is your day.' Paul thought she was just like his Auntie Brenda. Margaret's cheerful blonde attractiveness made everyone feel completely comfortable, while her portfolio of photographs of a thousand meetings like this one filled them with admiration.

'How do you do this all the time?' asked Marie.

'It's easy. Children like Paul are very special, and they deserve some happiness after what they've been through. It makes me happy to make them happy. They're my life, apart from my immediate family. I don't care about the rest,' she replied.

The publicists took the whole entourage down to the studios. And there were two of the most famous movie people in the world. From the back of the set, Spielberg looked diminutive, but there was no mistaking him. The boys were whisked off to meet him, speechless with excitement.

'Hi, guys,' said Spielberg as he greeted them. 'It's all in the imagination, you know. Anyone can do it. Sometimes I hate this job, but today is different. Do you play Dungeons and Dragons?' The conversation flowed for nearly an hour, the boys lapping up Spielberg's magic, talking about anything and everything.

Then in the distance, Paul could see a huge man striding towards them. At first Paul did not recognise him as he was so tall, but as he got closer, his face wreathed in smiles, Paul saw it was indeed Harrison Ford.

'You having a good time? Come and see the rats,' he said. At once the boys were off on another adventure. They saw the catacombs (complete with rats scurrying around them, spiders and webs), make-up and wardrobe, special effects and cameras. It all seemed a long way from Liverpool.

'Which part of Scotland you from?' joked Harrison Ford. 'I love the accent.' Margaret and Marie looked on, proud of the moment and enjoying the atmosphere. 'Which one's your Mum?' he asked. 'Let's say hallo to her too.' And for another three-quarters of an hour, the Sullivans from Liverpool enjoyed the company of one of the most highly prized actors in Hollywood.

The day sped by, and after an Italian lunch, it was time to go home. Paul had decided he was going to be a special effects technician, Marie had fallen for Harrison Ford, and everyone had enjoyed their day. 'I'll never ever forget it – none of us will,' Paul summed up.

*

Dreams Come True

The Parkers from East Ham in London will never forget their special day either. Their daughter Joanne, had also come through a two-year battle with leukaemia. From the age of four, she had been in and out of hospital undergoing the discomforts of chemotherapy and radiotherapy. Jill and Ken Parker had managed to soothe their little girl with cuddly toys, but by far her favourite was her soft Care Bear. She loved it, and it went everywhere with her and was her greatest friend. After the radiotherapy, Joanne's hair fell out in handfuls, but it was not long before it started to grow back again. Joanne was convinced that it was the Care Bears who had made that happen, and she loved them even more.

Jill had heard about Dreams Come True through the hospital, and decided to write to Margaret Hayles to see if she could arrange a treat for Joanne. She would so love to meet the Care Bears, so that she could thank them for making her hair grow again.

It was late March 1987, and Joanne, now six, was fit and well again, although she still had to have regular check-ups. Margaret telephoned the Parkers, and told them that a bus would collect the whole family on 9 April, for a special day out. Jill Parker went out and bought a new party dress for her daughter, and told her father and some very close friends to get ready for the big day. The jolly party was driven to The Royal Botanic Gardens in Kew, and were taken to the door of the Temperate House, a huge glass-vaulted Victorian building completely filled with magnificent tropical trees and flowers. The Parkers did not know what to expect next. Margaret greeted them, full of laughter, and gave little Joanne a big hug. Then she led her to an area that had been cordoned off, where a delicious picnic had been laid out.

Joanne's eyes grew wide. There were jellies and Smarties, sandwiches and trifles, lemonade and crisps – all her favourite goodies. Everyone tucked in, not really sure what was going to happen next, but having a lovely time anyway. Then suddenly Margaret nudged Joanne. 'Joanne, look over there. My goodness, what is it?' There was a cry of delight. For clambering towards them through the foliage was a gigantic pink Care Bear.

Joanne jumped to her feet, and the Care Bear cuddled her. 'Thank you for making my hair grow back,' she whispered, a little overcome by it all. Then it was party time. The children stuffed all manner of sweets and sandwiches into the creature's mouth, and when they felt the Care Bear had had enough, they skipped and ran together with her up and down the walkways of the Temperate House.

'Her face was a delight when she saw that bear,' remembers Jill. 'She'll never forget it, and I won't either.'

'There was a time when we thought we'd lose Joanne,' added Ken, 'but to see her like this today, well, I can't believe it. It's incredible. It's the happiest day of her life, and of ours.'

There was more fun, but soon it was time to go home. Joanne slept like a baby in the bus after her picnic, clutching a child-sized replica of her surprise friend. These days, each time she brushes her long hair, she smiles a wistful smile, remembering her day, and the pink bear who made it so special.

For Margaret, it was yet another success — one of more than a thousand — and a way for a whole family to relieve the horrors of a serious illness, a big boost for a recovering child, and another Dream Come True.

But life has not always been so rewarding for Margaret. Nobody knows exactly what happened in the first few days of her life, but her own story is like a fairy tale.

2

Margaret's Story

Margaret was found in Stockwell underground station in South London during the blitz. Nothing is known of her start in life, except that a kind woman called Jean found the tiny new-born child, and took her to the local children's home. The staff named the baby Jean Stockwell.

Little Jean was a favourite, and grew into a pretty infant. Her eyes remained clear blue and twinkled happily, while her hair was a mass of white-blonde curls. A year after Jean arrived at the home, Matron received a telephone call from George Farrer-Brown, an executive with the Bank Of Greece and Athens, who lived in Sussex. He explained that he and his wife had one adopted daughter already, aged seven. Perhaps Matron could think of a baby who also needed a home? Within just a few days Jean was adopted by the wealthy Farrer-Browns.

Back in Sussex, it took no time at all to settle in. George and Olive Farrer-Brown, both in middle age, had taken on a nanny for her. Jean's new home was called

Roselands, in Wivelsfield Green. It was a large brick house, set in beautiful gardens in the heart of Sussex. There were two acres of land, with tall fir trees and lots of flowers. Jean was soon renamed Margaret, a name felt to be much prettier.

The family moved to Hurstwood when Margaret was five. Their new home was early Victorian (a big, square white building, with tall windows and balconies) and was also set in several acres of idyllic countryside. There were stables, with a pony for the girls to ride and two donkeys, one of which had a foal. There was a chicken run at the back of the house, which meant a constant supply of eggs, a great treat in those times of rationing.

But although Margaret wanted for nothing material in those days, she was a lonely little girl. Her sister Shirley was much older, and her parents were busy running a home for the mentally handicapped. This meant that while both girls were left very much to their own devices in the splendid countryside, at the beginning and end of every term Margaret was dressed in her prettiest frock with a big bow in her hair, to be shown-off to the parents coming to deliver, or collect their children. She was installed in the kitchen with her nanny, and each time a different parent arrived, her mother would call out: 'Margaret dear, come and say hallo to Lady Riley' ... 'Lady Perrin' ... 'Mrs Sutherland'. The only advantage, as far as Margaret could see, was the extra biscuits and cakes she got to eat while waiting.

Margaret's best friends during her childhood were the

gardener Hubert Swatilla, a Polish refugee in his early twenties, who would push the small girl around in his wheelbarrow and let her feed the chickens, and her nanny Miss Annie Stanley.

Margaret was constantly ill with tonsillitis, and each time she recovered, she would become reinfected. Eventually, the doctor decided to remove them and she was admitted to Haywards Heath Cottage Hospital. She was very ill after the operation, and haemorrhaged; Margaret can still remember a tube being put up her nose to aspirate her. The doctors told her mother that she might not live the night. It took several months of constant care to recover, and Margaret spent the summer months dozing in a hammock in the garden as she got stronger.

After a short spell at a private school in Burgess Hill, Margaret was sent to Trevelyan Private School in Haywards Heath, where she started to board. She was nearly seven, and she loved it. The other girls were fun and Margaret enjoyed their company, even though she missed her nanny, Nana. Miss Annie Stanley was already in late middle age when she was taken on to look after Miss Margaret, as the staff in the Farrer-Brown household were instructed to call her. Margaret remembers that Nana wrote to her every single week with news from home, and always remembered Christmas and birthdays. These were precious gifts to young Margaret, because although Nana had very little money, she gave freely of love and attention to the child.

At school Margaret realised that it was a relief to break

away from the constraints of being the charming golden-haired child of wealthy socialites. She was glad to get out of the claustrophobic atmosphere at home, feeling that there she was more an adorable asset to show off rather than a valued daughter.

Summers were spent in the Farrer-Browns' house in Bracklesham Bay. It was a white brick house, with parquet floors and a verandah looking out over the sea. Shirley would have her friends to stay, and would swim, while Margaret spent time with children her own age. At that time, the seven-year age gap between the sisters seemed huge, and the girls had little in common.

Margaret left Trevelyan at 11, and continued her boarding school life at The Warren School in Worthing. She was very happy there too, although she was not an academic success. Margaret was a real tomboy and adored sport. But she was always in trouble for one thing or another, for climbing trees or swinging on the pipes in the dormitory. However, she did not always get caught. One night Matron came into the dormitory to check on the girls before lights out. She did her head count, and one was missing. 'Where is Margaret Farrer-Brown?' she demanded. 'She must be in the lavatory,' chirped the girls. But not at all. Margaret had climbed into the girders of the high ceiling, and was crouched there hiding from grumpy Matron. She got away with that incident, but there were others. Matron once even summoned her mother to the school because Margaret had decided not to wear her vest, and had hidden it under her mattress.

Margaret would sneak into the stables to see the ponies, knowing that if she was caught she would be reported. After six reports house colours were taken away, and Margaret was no stranger to being stripped of her house colours in front of the school. That meant no team sports, whether it was inter-house or inter-school, for two weeks. For the sports-mad Margaret, it was a painful punishment.

She hated studying and it was no surprise that, by 16, Margaret had not passed a single examination. Her parents felt they were wasting money on their daughter's education and decided to remove her from school. At this news Margaret cried her eyes out; she had been happier there than anywhere and wanted to stay.

Margaret was sent to Germany to stay with a family with the aim of learning the language. But she found post-war Germany frightening, and wrote home every day asking to be allowed to return to Sussex. Three months later she came back. Her mother found her a job at a local kennel in Uckfield. But she hated it, and after four months she left.

Margaret did not know what she wanted to do, but after a three-week spell at home, she knew she had to do something. She had never had an easy relationship with her mother, who was by now in her late sixties, and the atmosphere was tense. Margaret was 17, but was not allowed out on her own at night, wear make-up or have boyfriends. One day, she told her mother she was going into town shopping, but in fact went to Haywards Heath Cottage Hospital to see Matron Savage. A tall, thin grey-haired woman, with her hair tied in a bun, she took to Margaret immediately. In those days, they were crying out for nurses, and Matron asked Margaret to start straight away. She booked a taxi, went home and packed her bag. As she was leaving, she simply told her mother that she was off to become a nurse.

It was a very happy time as Margaret made lots of friends, and developed her love of traditional jazz, which she enjoys still. On Sunday evenings, Margaret and her friends would go to the local jazz club to hear the New City Jazzmen. They would go up to London to hear Ken Colyer and Chris Barber at the 100 Club, and when they were not listening to jazz, they were at parties.

Pam Hughes, a local hairdresser, became Margaret's closest friend. They met through the youth club, and became inseparable. They would head up to London, or go to Brighton together. Pam would tell her parents that she was staying with Margaret, and Margaret would tell Matron she was staying with Pam. One night in the summer, the girls ended up after a party sleeping on a park bench, listening to jazz singer Mahalia Jackson on Pam's radio, too embarrassed to admit they had nowhere to go. Luckily a friendly policeman found them, and they spent the rest of the night in the police station, drinking cups of tea and laughing. Pam eventually married a successful builder, and had four children. Tragically, she died suddenly from a brain haemorrhage in July 1986, two weeks after Margaret had visited her.

During those early pleasant days there was not too

much time for study, but Margaret scraped by, and after a year, she was sent to Cuckfield Hospital to start her nursing training proper. Margaret's social life became more hectic, and she learnt to exist on five hours sleep a night. But she began to find nursing depressing, and felt unable to cope with illness day in and day out. Hating to see people suffer, she also became increasingly upset when they died. Eighteen months into her training she quit.

It was while working on the perfume counter at Bourne and Hollingsworth in Oxford Street in London that Margaret fell in love for the first time. Tim Bearman was the local rugby hero, a tall, handsome, successful young man who worked on the metal exchange. Over a year later Margaret discovered she was pregnant, and on 24 March 1962 Margaret and Tim were married in Epsom. No expense was spared on the huge family affair, complete with top hats and frilly dresses. Margaret remembers feeling sick throughout the day as she was three months pregnant, and the fuss and attention was almost too much to bear.

It was not a happy marriage. There were four children within five years and her husband's earlier rugby club lifestyle did not alter with the addition of a wife and children. After thirteen painful years, the marriage broke down.

In 1975 Margaret married Tim Hayles, an architectural technician. Sadly the pressures of a ready-made family, and the close proximity of Margaret's first husband, eventually proved too much and the marriage collapsed after five years. While Tim Two was kindness itself, Margaret recognises in retrospect that she must have been impossible to live with.

Margaret was now alone with four children to look after.

3

Humble Beginnings

It was the start of a tough time for Margaret and her family. There was never quite enough money to go around, and Margaret was deeply depressed as, with no qualifications to speak of, she was unable to find work. It was March 1982, and Margaret walked the streets of Haywards Heath, looking for a job and trying to forget her desperate situation.

It was on one of these walks that by chance she bumped into her sister Shirley in the High Street. As they were talking, Shirley's neighbour, Doreen King, joined them. She had a daughter called Stephanie, aged 11, who was suffering from cancer, and who was feeling very sorry for herself, having just undergone rigorous chemotherapy. Her hair had fallen out, and she was very poorly. After talking for a few minutes, it transpired that Stephanie's greatest wish was to meet the Grand National champion jockey Bob Champion. He had had cancer, and had fought it and won.

After that meeting, Margaret began to put her life in perspective. Even if she was alone now, at least she and her four children were healthy. She worried about Stephanie, and thought long and hard about her dream to meet Bob Champion. Poor child, surely she deserved some happy moments amongst all the suffering?

Margaret resolved to call Bob up. She contacted her local horse trainer, Josh Gifford, to get Bob's phone number. When she rang, Bob agreed at once to meet Stephanie, and the following week, Margaret took the little girl to Fontwell Race Course in Sussex, where Bob was riding. Everyone was thrilled with the meeting. And for Stephanie, it really was a dream come true.

The local paper, the *Evening Argus*, ran the story. They published a photograph of Stephanie with Bob Champion with the headline 'Mrs Fixit Makes Child's Dream Come True'.

Margaret was amazed that something so simple could bring so much happiness. Stephanie King grasped a new lease of life, inspired by the courage and determination of Bob Champion. She too fought the fight and won. Today, six years on, Stephanie is a happy and attractive 18-year-old, without a trace of the cancer which had threatened her life.

Within a few days of the story's appearance in the *Argus*, Margaret received a letter from John and Linda Law from Brighton, whose son Danny had a brain tumour. The child wanted to meet Barry Sheene; the motor cycle ace was the embodiment of everything the 11-year-old aspired to. It so happened that Barry Sheene drank in Margaret's local hotel, and one evening she simply asked him if he would agree to meet Danny. Barry was thrilled to be asked and within a few minutes had arranged that Margaret should bring the child's whole family over to Barry's home for an afternoon.

It was a wonderful outing, and one which Margaret remembers with great fondness. It was crisp and cold, but Danny was delighted with the day. Barry took Danny for a ride, and after several hours of laughter, Barry and his family bid the Laws farewell. Danny was very ill at the time, and doctors thought that he might not make the outing at all. As it turned out, he made a miraculous recovery, and now he's a healthy and contented young man.

Margaret received another letter from a mother in Bristol, whose 14-year-old daughter had leukaemia. Trudy Beynon was very ill, but wanted to meet the actress Claire Grogan, who had starred in the film *Gregory's Girl*, and who sang with the pop group Altered Images. Margaret rang her agent, and within a few hours, Claire had agreed to take the train to Bristol with Margaret to see Trudy.

Margaret explained on the train how ill Trudy was, and Claire was in tears. She had come bearing gifts: the hat she wore in Trudy's favourite film, and cassettes and clothes. The Beynon family enjoyed the lunch, and Trudy was over the moon to meet Claire. Her parents said later that their daughter had not smiled and laughed so much in months.

It was a painful trip home, with both Margaret and Claire aware of the fragility of life. Three days later, brave Trudy Beynon passed away.

4

The Word Spreads

By late 1982, Dreams Come True – or the Sick Children's Celebrity foundation as it was then called – was taking off. Word was getting around that Mrs Fixit made miracles happen. She could make a sick child happy by fulfilling his or her dream; and there was no end of children.

Margaret had kept in touch with the Kings and the Laws, and would visit the children in hospital. One day, she was visiting Stephanie at Great Ormond Street Hospital in London, when the mother of the child in the next bed struck up a conversation. Mrs Saxton had heard about Stephanie's day with Bob Champion, and her little boy Andrew, aged six, who had leukaemia, was a great football fan. More than anything else, he wanted to meet soccer star Trevor Brooking who played for West Ham United. Andrew ended up spending a whole day with Trevor Brooking – a charming and very gentle man – and was treated like a prince. He came away with club shirts and scarves, and wonderful memories, and the renewed courage to fight on. Andrew won the fight, and made a full recovery.

Though working hard to make other people happy, Margaret's personal life was about to enter choppy waters. While raising money for a children's cancer fund with an ambitious project to take a party to Switzerland, Margaret found herself at serious cross-purposes with one of the project's sponsors. This resulted in a legal wrangle which forced Margaret to sell her small flat to repay the sponsor's £750 contribution.

Margaret was distraught at this turn of events. She did not know what to do, or where to turn. Lindsay, her eldest child, was nearly 18 by now, and was sent to stay with her father. The other three – Mandy, Jonathan and Nikki – moved into a local hotel with their mother. For the eight weeks until the money ran out, Margaret and the three kids, now 16, 15 and 13, lived on top of each other in one room at the Bent Arms Hotel in Lindfield, feeling under pressure and bickering away like mad.

Margaret went for help to the council, who placed her and the children in a house for the homeless in Burgess Hill. Parkside no longer exists, but Margaret remembers it as the most dreadful place. The family lived alongside all sorts of strange people: addicts, drunks and thieves shouted at each other all night in nearby rooms. There was no choice but to stay there and three months went by when one ghastly incident followed another. There were fights in the other rooms, and the children were threatened. Finally, Margaret felt they had to leave, no matter what. She sent Mandy to join her father, and Jonathan to her sister. She kept Nikki, the youngest, with her, and together mother and daughter spent the next six months in a cold and damp rented room in Cuckfield.

The following three months were brightened a little when Margaret and Nikki were able to stay at a friend's house. But a terrible blunder meant that £7,000 worth of furniture, which Margaret had stored while she looked for a permanent home, was taken away by the council. Margaret was struck a double blow when she realised that it had all been uninsured and she could get no compensation for her loss. Unable to solve her accommodation problems, Margaret and Nikki were forced to spend the next uncomfortable year living out of suitcases in a variety of places, never being quite sure what was going to happen next.

Luckily everything was not all doom and gloom, for by this time, Margaret had met an engraver called Simon Callagan, with whom she was spending a great deal of time. He was immensely supportive of her work, and offered to let her share his tiny workroom in Haywards Heath. It held his engraving machine, one chair and a work bench. There was a telephone, and Margaret wrote letters on her knee. When the phone rang, she had to kick Simon to stop the machine, so she could hold a conversation. If he had to use the polisher, Margaret would have to move out of the chair. For a year, this was the nerve centre of Dreams Come True.

Eventually problems with illegally sub-letting landlords, at a rented house they had to share with nine other people, became so acute that Margaret sent Nikki to stay with a school friend. Margaret had no choice but to spend a few nights sleeping in the car, which was on a year's loan to the charity, while she looked for a place to rent. At last she found a room in a house in Hurstpierpoint where, for the next year, she lived alone. But although it was warm and cosy, she was surrounded by alcoholics, drug addicts, religious freaks, and a girl who was emotionally disturbed, and screamed, cried and fought with her husband.

As an escape from her housing difficulties Margaret threw herself into work, and Dreams Come True thrived from Simon's workroom. Terminally ill children still had wishes, and Margaret put great faith in the charity motto *Numquam Desiste* (Never Give Up), believing the children must never give up fighting for life, and she must never give up working for their happiness.

By now it was late 1985, and finally Margaret's life took a turn for the better. A marketing firm heard about Dreams Come True, and decided to sponsor Margaret for a year. The sponsorship was the turning point of Dreams Come True; it meant that at last Margaret could rent a house in Cuckfield so that she could have an office and secretary, and her children could be together again. With the day-to-day running of the charity sorted out Margaret was able to give Simon back his workshop. Her relationship with this softly-spoken man had blossomed, and his love and support continue still to give her the strength she needs to carry on.

The requests were pouring in by now, as word of Dreams Come True spread throughout the country. Then Margaret had a brainwave: she would take a group of children to the Montreux Rock Festival. There had been lots of requests to meet several pop stars such as Paul Young, Spandau Ballet, Tears for Fears and Duran Duran. After numerous telephone calls, Duran Duran's agent came back to Margaret and suggested that as the band was out of the country for most of the coming few months, why not catch up with them in Montreux?

Margaret thought it was a great idea. This way she could make several children's dreams come true at the same time. Schools Abroad, a firm which specialises in arranging group trips, helped by organising the accommodation, and soon a merry throng was on its way to the small Alpine village of Leysin, nestled in the hills above Montreux, in Switzerland. Each child brought a parent on the trip, and there were two nurses in attendance from the hospitals that Margaret was now dealing with on an almost weekly basis. It was a jolly group, and was by far the most ambitious project she had taken on. The party consisted of 12 youngsters, 12 mums, two nurses, Margaret and her two helpers, Simon, and her daughter Nikki. It was quite a crowd to organise, but a more excited band of travellers would have been hard to find. Throughout the journey there was the sound of happy laughter. Montreux was idyllic, set on the shores of Lake Geneva, and the children were delighted. It was bright and sunny, and the town of Montreux itself was humming, with tourists and rock fans from all over the world thronging its streets.

Sarah Dando from Bristol had wanted to meet Duran Duran for years. The brave 15-year-old had been in hospital a great deal that year with cystic fibrosis, an incurable disease which makes it very difficult to breathe because of increased mucus in the chest. Also it affects the digestion because certain chemicals simply are not made by the body. The patient often has to take up to 20 tablets, six or seven times a day, and has to undergo rigorous physiotherapy to facilitate breathing. Throughout the often painful treatment, Sarah had listened to cassettes of her favourite band. Her mother had written to Margaret several weeks before, explaining that Sarah's condition was deteriorating, and that she might not survive the illness which had been with her from birth. To be able to look forward to something like a meeting with Duran Duran would certainly give her the encouragement she needed to keep on fighting.

Two other Duran Duran fans were Amanda Eddy, from Cornwall, and Lisa Cummings, from Wiltshire. They were both lovely 15-year-old girls, who were suffering from cancer. Like Sarah, they had undergone painful and unpleasant treatment that year, and the thought of meeting their favourite rock stars had strengthened them through the last few weeks of treatment.

On the morning of the meeting, the girls anxiously put on their trendiest clothes, and set off to the stadium. When they met the band, the girls were all thrilled, and cried with the excitement of the day. Each was given mementoes of the most exciting day they had ever had.

Lyndsay Dutfield, from Chichester, had longed to meet Paul Young, and this was to be her golden moment too. At 21, Lyndsay had leukaemia, and had been very ill for some time. The thought of talking with her favourite star had cheered her, and on this trip she was more energetic and happy than her mother could remember. It was a delightful meeting, with the pop star taking over an hour out of his schedule to sit and chat with Lyndsay. She was delighted, and although she was very ill, it perked her up no end.

Paul was equally delighted with the meeting, and with the whole concept of Dreams Come True. It was 1986, and he was at the height of his career, having had several hit records. He wanted to do as much as he could for Margaret, and he offered financial support to the charity. Not only would he pay Margaret's salary for a time, he agreed to become a patron, and to meet as many children as possible.

Paul's gesture, and indeed the trip itself, were both food for thought for Margaret, and on the way back to England a week later, she had time to reflect on the success of the trip. The offer of help came at exactly the right moment, as the previous sponsor had pledged one year's support and that year was almost up. For the charity to survive, it needed generous donations, and this one was perfect.

Back in England, the kids from Montreux dined out on their stories, and Margaret vowed that Dreams Come True would go each year. But some of those who had been on that first trip would not see another. Lyndsay Dutfield lived for a year, and died eventually from her leukaemia in considerable pain; her mother Liz has remained a close friend of Margaret's. Sarah Dando finally succumbed to the cystic fibrosis which had wracked her small body since birth. But both Amanda Eddy and Lisa Cummings are well, and appear to be winning the fight against cancer.

The group holidays became more and more popular. It was a great way for Margaret to see several children fulfil their dreams at once. For many of those on the Dreams Come True trips, it is the first time both children and parents have had the chance to leave not only the UK, but in many cases, their home town. These illnesses mean that families are tied to the hospital where the child receives his or her treatment, and long spells away are costly and nerve-racking. Margaret aims to relieve some of the pressure of the daily grind for the whole family by giving them something to look forward to.

There have now been four trips to Montreux, and these days, the Swiss National Tourist Office lays on all sorts of days out for the party. The members of the group all travel by coach to Paris, where they spend their first night; everyone dines out in style and rides to the top of the Eiffel Tower to get a really good view of the French capital. The next day, the party leaves for Switzerland and the Hostellerie des Chevaliers Gruyères, a huge chalet high in the hills above Montreux run by a charming Swiss lady called Simone Boucherie, who fusses over everyone from morning until night, cooking fabulous meals, preparing picnics for their outings, and at the end of the stay, she throws a party. No child goes home empty-handed. Swiss chocolate, cow bells, Alpine hats and flowers accompany each one, and are reminders of their fantastic time. The parents benefit from the chance to see their children relax and enjoy themselves. The rock festival has concerts on each of its five nights, and Margaret makes sure the kids get to at least three. The rest of the visit is spent sight-seeing and picnicking in the spectacular countryside.

Bob Cole, a travel agent in Rainham who accompanied one of the trips, observes: 'I actually think that the mental anguish of the parents sometimes outweighs the physical torment of the children. These trips go a long way to making life a little more normal.'

One mum, Anne Payne from Bristol, would have a little weep each morning. She went to Montreux in 1987 with her 21-year-old son Richard, a cystic fibrosis sufferer. Because Richard had been so ill all his life, they had never been out of Bristol, and she could not believe they were actually there. 'This trip was one of the happiest times of my life. I had never seen Richard so happy, and to take away the pressure of caring for him at home was a huge relief. We never stopped laughing.' Richard died six months after his return but Anne says she will always remember Richard as he was in Switzerland – full of joy and with a sparkle in his eye that had chased away the pain.

The year before, Louise Balhatchet's parents shared those feelings. Louise's nightmare began a few weeks before her thirteenth birthday, when she had not been feeling well. She was tired, run down, and was losing a great deal of weight. Breathing was difficult, and she had some pains in her sides. But perhaps more revealing was the soreness of her mouth. The gums were bruised and bleeding, and she had a mouth full of ulcers.

Shirley Balhatchet took her daughter to the GP, who thought she had a heart murmur, and referred her at once to the John Radcliffe Hospital in Oxford. Shirley was very anxious, hardly daring to think what might be wrong with Louise, a calm and gentle girl with an ability to make people laugh even in the most difficult situations. The heart specialist examined Louise, and was concerned about both the x-rays, and her symptoms. In addition, he could see fluid round her heart, and told Shirley and Dash Balhatchet that if Louise had not been admitted there and then, she would have died before nightfall from the build-up of pressure. She was put straight to bed, but still he was not satisfied. He called another specialist, the onco-logist Dr John Montcrieff, who looked anxiously at Louise's mouth. Shirley was beginning to fear the worst.

She had a friend whose son had leukaemia, and when she overheard the doctors talking about bone marrow she began to tremble. 'Don't worry, Mum,' said Louise, 'I'm in very good hands here, I'll be all right.'

Within a couple of hours, tests had been processed, but Louise seemed to know already. 'I've got leukaemia, haven't I?' she said. Indeed she had, and it was a most virulent strain. It was 6 December 1985, and Louise was to undergo immediate treatment. 'We were shattered,' remembers Shirley. 'We just couldn't believe it. Equally, we had no idea what to expect, and the next few weeks were horrific for Louise and for us.'

Louise had chemotherapy and radiotherapy. For nine weeks, the child stayed in hospital, alternating between the nausea and depression caused by the intense course of drugs, and the soreness caused by the radiation. Throughout the sordid business, however, she remained calm. Sometimes, she would cry a little, but she would always protect her parents' feelings. 'Don't worry about me, I'm just having a down day today,' she said.

After nine weeks, though still on radiation, she came home. She was glad to be back with her favourite cuddly toys, close to her younger sister Lisa, and surrounded by the warmth of her family and friends. But each time she had an infection, no matter how apparently insignificant, she was rushed back to hospital. Leukaemia victims have little resistance to infections, and the most minor ailments become very serious.

By this time it was March, and Louise's hair was falling

out. There were clumps of it on the pillow in the morning, and just stroking it would cause it to come out. There was nothing she could do, of course, as this was a side-effect of the treatment. But it did very little for her morale. She was coping, though, and she still managed to laugh and joke with her friends and doctors. When she was back in hospital with another infection, Shirley would occasionally arrive to see Louise putting make-up on the staff, making them look like clowns.

There was a nurse on the ward that Louise felt particularly close to, Marianne Middleton. Marianne had taken Louise under her wing, charmed by the child's ready laughter and bright smile. It would distress Marianne when Louise was feeling down, and after her hair fell out she was very low. Marianne had met Margaret Hayles before, as children from the John Radcliffe Hospital had been to Montreux the previous year and Marianne had been impressed by the way the trip helped the children. There was another Montreux coming up and she suggested Louise as a possible candidate.

Margaret agreed. When Marianne put it to her Louise replied, 'You're joking!' But her face was wreathed in smiles. She had been through the worst times and was ready for some fun. Shirley would go with her, and the doctors announced she was well enough to travel. Dr Montcrieff had told the Balhatchets that Louise would not survive a relapse; the leukaemia she suffered from was particularly strong, and there was no known cure. It was his view that while she was well, she should enjoy herself. The Balhatchets were delighted. Dash, a long-distance lorry driver, had given up his job when Louise had become ill, to be close to her and the rest of the family. There was no way that they could afford a holiday. Louise could not wait to dust off her autograph book, smarten up her wardrobe, and get going.

But only a few weeks before the trip, Louise found a lump under her arm. The family was panic-stricken, and felt as if time was running out fast. Louise, however, had great faith and felt sure that she would recover. The hospital decided to try to shrink the tumour using radiotherapy, and while the treatment was successful, Louise was very tender under her arm. But nothing was going to stop her, and sore arm or not, she had packed all her things and was ready to go in early May.

Louise had the time of her life. She loved Switzerland, the views took her breath away, and the other people in the group were great fun. And she loved Margaret, whom she met for the first time, and was never far from her side. Louise was a constant source of laughter. Shirley would come down in the mornings, and find Louise surrounded by other mums, chatting away. At the festival she met lots of stars: Paul Young, Phil Collins, The Eurythmics, Roger Daltrey, Billy Ocean, A-Ha, Julian Lennon and Queen. She spent hours talking and laughing, taking photographs, and telling everyone that it was not so bad to have leukaemia if you could go to Switzerland too. Louise returned to England with an autograph book bulging with new additions, full of memories, and determined that above everything else, she wanted to help Margaret. Louise felt strongly that other children should be able to enjoy trips like Montreux, and she wanted to help raise money for Dreams Come True.

But that lump had returned, and once again Louise went back into hospital for more radiotherapy. There were more injections and drugs, and again, she was nauseous and depressed. Margaret kept in touch, telephoning regularly to see how she was, and wondering what else she could do to cheer her up. Blackpool was on the list of trips. Margaret was to take children to see comedian Russ Abbott, a Dreams Come True favourite. Louise made sure she was well enough to travel, and as a bonus, when breakfast television decided to interview Margaret, Louise was on TV-AM too. She loved it, the publicity made her feel very special and she sparkled more than ever.

Four weeks later, Margaret was to take several teenagers to the Prince's Trust concert at Wembley. There were to be scores of famous stars performing in front of the Prince and Princess of Wales, many of whom had agreed to meet up with Margaret's entourage on the day. As Louise was so ill, it would do her no end of good to be part of that party. Since Montreux, only six weeks earlier, she had been through more rigorous and unpleasant treatment, and had tried hard to keep her spirts up. Louise was thrilled with the idea, and as the time approached, she would ring Margaret almost daily for an update on who would be there.

When the big day arrived, the Balhatchets climbed into the family car and drove down to London. It was a good day out for everyone, for Louise's illness had more than taken its toll on all members of the family. In Wembley they joined Margaret's party, and as it grew in size, the stars would come and go. For many, it was a renewal of a friendship started in Montreux. Paul Young remembered Louise: 'Not you again . . . you're looking good.' Phil Collins remembered her too, as did several others. But there were other stars there she had not met. David Bowie laughed and fooled around with Louise, who told him funny tales of incidents in hospital. They laughed like drains, and both were full of mischief. 'You're a cocky little thing, aren't you?' he joked, as Margaret snapped photos of them. Rod Stewart was enthralled by her too, and enjoyed the stories and good humour of this delightful child.

But as far as Louise was concerned, the best was yet to come. Her ultimate idol was to make an appearance, and she was more excited than she could imagine: George Michael did not have a great deal to time to spare, but he gave her a hug and lots of cassettes. Louise was over the moon, and after her return home, did not stop talking about the day in London. She went back into hospital almost immediately afterwards, and had the lump under her arm removed. But her hero had not forgotten her, and a telegram arrived at the hospital, bearing good wishes, and four tickets for his London concert. She was thrilled that George Michael had remembered her, and although she was still very ill indeed, the family made the pilgrimage to the concert, and thoroughly enjoyed it.

But it was all too much, and Louise was weaker and weaker. She begged to be taken home, and in mid-September, with pain killers for comfort, she was installed in her own room at home. On 17 September, a Wednesday, she told her parents that she was ready to leave them now. 'I'm going to die, but please don't worry, you'll be able to cope. I did try to fight, I really did, but I'm just too tired.' Three days later Louise Balhatchet died. Her parents conclude: 'No amount of money could make up for the pleasure Louise had from her time in Montreux. Those are memories we will carry with us for the rest of our lives.'

Lee Hooley from Manchester had a great time in Montreux. Lee was 15 when he became ill, in September 1985. He had been limping, and gradually over a period of months he lost the use of his right side. He laughs now, but at the time, he says he looked drunk. His schoolmaster called him aside one day and accused him of glue sniffing, but an observant nurse thought the boy was not well. Lee's mother Janet Davey was called to the school, and he was taken to the local hospital.

It did not take long for the doctor to see what was wrong, and after sending Lee and his step-father Howard Davey from the room, the doctor explained to Janet that Lee possibly had a brain tumour. She emerged from the doctor's room in tears, and Lee was shocked. 'Mum explained that I had a trapped nerve, and that I had to have an operation to unblock it. I never imagined for a minute that it was serious,' he remembers.

One week later, Lee had his first operation. It was Friday 13 September. The tumour was benign but was so large, and so near to the nerve centre, that it was inoperable. It was decided that Lee should be moved from Manchester Royal Infirmary to Christie's Hospital, for radiotherapy. After 15 days of treatment, he was discharged, and after several months of very frequent check-ups, Lee was back in good form. He started to exercise, and regained the use of the right side of his body. He was in high spirits, back at school, and all seemed well.

But the doctors decided that a shunt was necessary; this is a procedure which removes fluid from the brain and eases pressure. Exactly one year after the first operation, Lee was readmitted to hospital for what should have been a routine operation. The shunt was put in place, to drain fluid off the brain, and empty it into the stomach, to be expelled normally. But somehow, in the course of the operation, again Lee lost the use of the right side of his body. 'He lost the will to live then,' recalls his mother. 'He was so depressed that he'd got well, and then he was back to square one. It didn't seem fair.'

'I was ready to chuck it all in. I couldn't believe it, that after what I'd already been through, suddenly it was as if nothing had improved,' says Lee. Lee claims that it was the telephone call from Margaret that cheered him up. She had learned of his problems through the hospital, and with Montreux only a few weeks away, she thought it would cheer him up. 'It gave me something to look forward to, and really, the will to live,' says Lee. 'I stopped being sorry for myself, I just got up one morning, and started to exercise.'

Lee decided to take his step-father, Howard, with him on the trip. With five sisters, Lee and Howard were good mates and had a great time in Switzerland. He remembers sitting in the Hyatt Hotel in Montreux, and the stars trooping in. Margaret told him to stand up, and say hallo to singer Kim Wilde, and Lee gave her a very warm welcome with a huge kiss. He was the life and soul of the party and nobody could have imagined that this boy had been so ill.

On the last night, Lee and Howard disappeared from the chalet after everyone had gone to bed. They returned in the early hours of the morning with some trophies – two real cow bells complete with mud, which they had pinched from the necks of some very shocked Alpine cows. As a surprise for Margaret on the journey home, Lee presented one of the bells to her as a thank you. Simon had it gold plated and turned into a clock, and today the bell sits in pride of place on Margaret's desk.

Sean Steel shared the room with Lee and Howard. Sean was from Barnstaple in Devon. He had just turned 16 in 1984, when a fall from his bicycle on the way to work, laid him low. He badly knocked his knee and it refused to heal. Finally, after seeing the doctor, he was sent to Bristol Children's Hospital for a biopsy, where the lump on his knee was found to be cancerous.

Sean underwent chemotherapy, and bore up well to the painful treatment. He was wonderful with the other kids on the ward, for at 16, he was considerably older than they were. Sean rationalised the nausea by thinking of it as a hangover, but his hair fell out, and in spite of his courage, he was fed up. He had to go to Birmingham Children's Hospital for an operation on his leg; Dr Smeph had agreed to take him, to replace the knee with a metal joint. He was one of the few surgeons in the country to perform this operation, and Sean hoped that it would save his leg.

The operation was a success, and within a few weeks, Sean was mobile again. Only a slight limp gave away the fact that he had had an operation, and his mother remembers that three weeks after he came home, Sean cycled down to her shop to see her. When she asked how he had managed, he told her he'd made a loop on the handlebars from the strap on his lunch box, and had slung his leg through it. The rest was just gliding downhill.

But by November 1986, Sean was ill again and the doctors found secondary growths of cancer in his lungs. They operated, and he endured more chemotherapy. He was thoroughly fed up, but his friends tried to cheer him up. It was not all fun, though. Sean's appearance, still bald after the chemotherapy and considerably thinner, made some people uncomfortable. At the local disco one night, he was refused entry when the bouncer asked him to take off his hat. But these difficulties did not keep him down for long, his mother Jesse remembers. 'Sean kicked the arse out of life, he loved it, and never complained. He lived for each and every moment.'

Margaret rang the Steels up out of the blue, having heard about Sean through the hospital. It was Easter 1987, and Sean's treatment was due to continue till July. Would he be well enough to go to Montreux, she wanted to know? 'Yes', said Sean and Jesse, and the hospital arranged that Sean could take his medication with him. There would be highly-qualified nurses on the trip to care for him, and he knew what to expect. Soon they were on their way. 'For that period of time, there was nothing else on his mind but the rock festival. He was there to have a good time, and he did. I can see his smiling, laughing face. It means more to me than anything,' Jesse adds.

Sean loved it. He enjoyed meeting the celebrities, and they liked him. Margaret suggested he might like to have his photo taken with Samantha Fox, and Sean knew this would make him the envy of his best friend who was devoted to Sam and who had her pictures all over his room.

All good things have to end, and after the laughter of Montreux, Sean returned to Barnstaple. He was in the highest spirits, and was learning to drive. The summer sped by, and Sean lived life to the utmost. But in

September, he started to complain of discomfort in his side, and could hardly eat at all. The week after his birthday, in early September, he passed his test, and drove himself to the hospital for some routine x-rays. His left side was riddled with cancer, and once again Sean was back in a hospital bed, on radiotherapy. There was nothing more anyone could do, and so Jesse and Trevor Steel took their son home, to die. Mrs McCormack, his school teacher who had also fought cancer, came to visit him one day and asked him what he would most like to do. Sean replied that he wanted to have a party for all his friends. It was a fabulous party, and Sean said later that he had attended his own wake. Three days later, on 3 October 1987, Sean Steel passed away peacefully at home. His parents are eternally grateful to Margaret for making his last few months so happy. Their son's laughter in Montreux, and his unfailing good humour, right to the end, is their cherished memory.

Katherine Nadine, a 15-year-old from Worcester, had a particularly virulent and painful stomach tumour, and had spent most of the year in hospital. But the thought of her trip to Montreux had kept her going. Her mother, Heather, said it was truly extraordinary to see the way Katherine fought her illness to be able to go. 'For children like Katherine, treats of this kind mean more than any amount of medicine. Not only that, it is important for a child her age to realise that she isn't the only one who's lost her hair from the chemotherapy. It is good to be able to compare notes.' Katherine loved it and made many friends, returning home stronger and healthier.

Sometimes the dream trips do not end with Margaret Hayles's contribution. Michelle Bright, from Hull, enjoyed her trip to Montreux for, like the other children, this 13-year-old had undergone painful treatment for cancer. When she returned to Hull, the local paper ran her story. A kind-hearted neighbour, who had never realised how ill Michelle was, paid for her and her family to go to Disneyland.

And there are always romances on these trips, says Margaret. There is nothing like getting away from the pressures of home to make you start to take a renewed interest in your appearance, and to notice other people. For the single mums and dads, it is an opportunity to meet new people, and there have been several happy endings. There have been romances and new friendships, a bond between parents and children reinforced with mutual respect through suffering, and the simple joy of laughter and good cheer after so much pain and so many tears. One of the divorced mums fell in love with a courier on one of the trips, and they later married. Indeed, they named their house 'Dreams Come True'.

The success of Montreux has spurred Margaret on to come up with trips for younger children. Santa World, in Sweden, seemed a good idea; a Christmas trip for the whole family, and the dream of dreams for the little ones.

Lee Holmes, aged 12, summed it up. He had looked

forward to this trip for some time, having spent many months in hospital having treatment for a brain tumour. The tumour had left Lee with some intellectual damage, but he was a charming little boy. Lee just could not believe his eyes when he saw the brightly dressed Santa Claus for the first time, riding in his sleigh, with two reindeer alongside. 'My friends all told me that Santa Claus didn't exist. But now I've seen him for myself, I believe he does!' he exclaimed, to the amusement of all the other children.

Amy Wood, and sister Lucy, were also on that trip. It was something both girls had looked forward to for some time. Amy had become ill in January 1984, around the time of her third birthday. Her mother Julia had noticed that Amy simply was not paying attention, and more importantly, she did not seem to hear things. The GP told her that Amy had a build-up of catarrh in the inner ear, and shortly afterwards, she went down with mumps.

Amy's condition did not improve, and by June, the doctor was talking of removing her adenoids. A family holiday to the caravan in Wales was planned, and so any surgery was put off till their return. The Woods took off for Wales, and installed themselves on the picturesque Gower Coast. But Amy could not breathe at night, and would wake up every hour or so, and Julia and Colin Wood were increasingly anxious. Then they noticed something in Amy's nose. It looked like a peanut, but Julia knew it could not be one. 'I never allowed the children to have nuts. I'd heard so many dreadful stories of kids choking on them, that I banned them from the house.' She tried to remove it, but without luck. It would not budge. A local GP sent them to Swansea Hospital, and the casualty officer there could not remove it either.

Amy was referred to the Ear, Nose and Throat department, and x-rays revealed more than a peanut. They suggested that Amy return to Birmingham, to the Children's Hospital. The consultant had his suspicions, when he examined Amy on the Tuesday, and by Thursday she was admitted for an operation first thing on the Friday morning. It was 1 August, and the family was preparing for Lucy's fifth birthday party two days later.

Julia remembers the surgeon coming out of theatre, talking to several other parents, but disappearing before he spoke with her. Colin Wood, a police sergeant, had taken the day off, and once he had seen Amy safely out of theatre, he had gone to pick up his other daughter's birthday cake. Julia was called into the doctor's office, and the exchange was brief but shocking.

'Sit down. Mrs Wood. I have bad news, and there's no easy way to tell you this. Amy has a cancerous tumour.'

The 'peanut' they had all seen was in fact the tumour, which had grown down through the bone at the root of the nose. Amy had a 60/40 chance of survival, but treatment was to start as soon as possible. Amy was allowed to go home for the weekend, to celebrate her sister's birthday, but first thing on the Monday, after a tense and deeply anxious weekend, they were to be back for treatment.

A full body scan revealed that the tumour was contained at the back of the nose, but it was so close to the nerve centre of the brain that it was inoperable. The oncologist, Dr Jillian Mann, prescribed chemotherapy and radiotherapy, and it was to start at once. Julia left her job, unable to maintain it and look after Amy. They sold the family car, and bought an old runabout, and eventually, with money so short, they sold their home, and bought a small town house so that Julia could be with Amy.

Amy tolerated her treatment beautifully. They made a mask to protect her face and head from the radiotherapy, and the little mite would lie on the table, remaining perfectly still. Then she would lift her right hand and wave, then her left hand, and then both, and wave at the nurses she knew were watching. When her hair started to fall out, she made little jokes about it. She had a toy rabbit, and one day, she put it on her head. 'What are you doing that for?' asked her mother. 'This is the hare on my head!' replied Amy.

In January 1985, a year since Amy was first ill, Dr Mann founded SPOCC, the Society of Parents of Children with Cancer. Julia was to be the secretary, and within a few weeks, she was busily fund-raising. Then she saw Margaret on TV-AM, who by now had given her a car and plenty of air-time. Julia wrote, telling her about SPOCC, and within a few days, Margaret was on the phone. Together, they planned several outings for children in Birmingham, and the ball was rolling.

Margaret wanted to know who Amy would like to

meet, and the answer was a great surprise. Margaret Thatcher and Father Christmas were her favourites. Julia did not give it a thought assuming it would all be too hard. But Margaret wasn't daunted. Father Christmas would not be a problem as there was another Santa World trip planned already. But Mrs Thatcher might be harder, especially as it was election year. She thought about it, and decided that she would get in touch with her local MP, Timothy Renton. Margaret set about fixing the meeting. She telephoned his office, but could not get through. A letter was sent off, and followed up by several more telephone calls. It was late April by now, and the election was set for 11 June. Margaret was determined that Mrs Thatcher would see Amy soon, and finally the letter she had waited for came through. Mrs Thatcher would be delighted to have some afternoon tea with the Woods on 7 May.

Everyone was in their best clothes. Amy had a new dress, blue check with a white lace collar, and her hair was growing back now, in beautiful blond curls. The girls had decided to take gifts for the Thatchers. Amy had wrapped a Nottingham lace handkerchief in pink tissue paper for Mrs Thatcher, and Lucy had an Irish linen one, wrapped in blue tissue, for Denis Thatcher.

The group met at the Foreign Office; Timothy Renton was to be their guide and would spend the day with them. They had a tour of the corridors of power, the high ceilings and the magnificent cornicing greatly impressing the older Woods. The girls loved the Foreign Office too –

the long corridors were a delight to run down at full speed.

They came out of the Foreign Office by the back door, and there was Number Ten almost directly opposite. A quick photograph with the policeman on duty, and the Woods were ushered inside. The girls were so excited. They took another photograph by the fireplace where Mr Reagan and Mr Gorbachev had talked with the Prime Minister, and then they were ushered into the Blue Room to wait for their host. At four o'clock, Mrs Thatcher arrived. The room filled with her presence, but in moments she had put everyone at ease. 'You must be Amy,' she said, gently shaking the child's little hand, 'and you must be Lucy.' They chatted for several minutes, and then the tea was served. It was a magnificent cake, in the shape of a ballot box.

'I've been looking for someone special to share this with,' she said. 'I can't think of anyone more special than you.' And with that, she gave everyone a huge piece of cake. Suddenly, she snatched Amy's back from her. 'This won't make her ill, will it?' she asked Julia anxiously. 'No, she'll be just fine,' was the relieved answer. The cake was returned, and Mrs Thatcher spread tissues on the children's laps, so they would not mark their dresses.

With the election coming up, Mrs Thatcher had to rush off to a meeting, but she did not let the children leave empty-handed. She went up to her private apartments and returned with a Crown Derby figurine for each child, a chipmunk and a rabbit. Then she handed Amy a huge teddy, on behalf of Dreams Come True, but so that Lucy would not feel left out, she dashed back upstairs again, and came back with a teddy bear wearing a tie for Lucy, who immediately called it Denis. Looking back now, Amy is still thrilled that such a busy person should have taken half an hour to meet her.

Santa World was up and coming though, planned for early December. It was to be a family affair, as Margaret wanted parents and brothers and sisters to have some fun together. So often, when one child in a family is ill, the others feel neglected and left out. A trip like this one was an opportunity for everyone to be involved, and so as December approached, the whole Wood family was looking forward to their time away. As the day of departure loomed ahead, Amy and Lucy became more and more excited. Amy was undergoing some treatment, and even the doctors were impressed with the way the determined child coped.

'I must be well enough for Doctor to let me go to see Santa,' she said as she silently bore the discomfort. And she was. On the morning of 5 December, a group of children and their parents left the Birmingham Children's Hospital by coach, and headed down to London. There they met up with the Dreams Come True bus and were soon on their way. There were videos on the bus, and lots of lemonade and chocolate for everyone to indulge in. On the second day, they arrived in Sweden. The Dreams Come True Bus was decked out in streamers and Christmas decorations, with balloons and toys hanging from every overhead rack and seat. The film *Santa Claus* was playing on the video, and parents and children were having a great time.

The next day, they arrived at Mora in Sweden. In the middle of nowhere, it seemed, in the late afternoon, like a chocolate-box cover to look at. The next morning, bright and early, everyone was up, on the coach, and heading for Santa World. And there in the heart of the Swedish countryside, with fir trees peeking above the snow and reindeer grazing nearby, was Santa's own little house.

Amongst gasps of oohs and aahs, the children and their families piled off the bus, and made their way across the snow to Santa's house. The elves were busily at work, packing up the presents that Santa Claus would take with him on his travels. His cat was curled up by the big open fire, and the sledges were nearby, ready for the off. It was quite breathtaking, and everyone, old and young, was thoroughly charmed by it. Each child sat with Santa, and told him their secret wishes and had their photograph taken. By five o'clock, they were tired, but very happy, and ready to return to the hotel for supper and carols.

Not every child on the trip was ill, however. Others were taken as a reward to the families who had been through so much. Mrs Holt, from Lancing, was there with her healthy son; her daughter had died at the age of eight only a few weeks before. Mrs Holt had so looked forward to the trip that Margaret thought it would help her cope with her bereavement to come along.

Margaret Brittain, from Coventry, was in the same

position. Her daughter Paula had died, also aged eight, of cancer. But she was represented by her brother Mark and her sister Anna, who both had a great time. For them it was a welcome relief from the sadness of their sister's illness and death. Margaret Hayles has always maintained that the whole family should benefit from Dreams Come True, as when a child is ill the whole family suffers too.

Another child who got a big kick out of Santa World was five-year-old Tyrone Campbell from Hackney in London. Tyrone and his mother Janet loved every single moment of the trip, and from the minute they left their home, they were having fun. Tyrone enjoyed the coach ride, the ferry, sitting on Santa's lap, a sledge ride, petting the reindeer and watching the elves at work; it was almost more than he could bear. For Janet, it was a much-needed break from the daily grind of life, and a real boost to her morale.

Tyrone had already fulfilled another dream earlier in the year. The little boy had first become ill in June 1985, when Janet noticed that he simply was not himself. He could not walk far and he had no appetite. Janet took him to her GP three times, and he sent her away, saying that the child had a throat infection which would clear up. She also took him to the casualty department of her local hospital, Queen Elizabeth's, in Hackney, five times before they would admit him. They had run blood tests, and could find nothing wrong. But on the fifth occasion, the doctor noticed that Tyrone's tummy was very distended. After examining him, she admitted him, because his kidneys felt enlarged. The kidney specialist from Great Ormond Street was visiting the hospital, and after his examination, he recommended that Tyrone be moved at once to Great Ormond Street. Janet felt herself panic because as a single parent she had nobody to turn to for support, and Tyrone was her only child.

After extensive tests, Janet Campbell was told that Tyrone, who was two and a half, had a tumour on each of his kidneys. A lumbar puncture to sample the bone marrow would reveal what kind of tumours they were. In fact, Tyrone had leukaemia, but his blood had not revealed this yet, and because of Tyrone's dark skin, the bruising was not visible. Janet was stunned.

Tyrone started extra-strong cranial radiotherapy, because already the leukaemia had infiltrated his spine, but he was always very sick afterwards. The chemotherapy suited the plucky little boy better, and he soon started to improve. Janet was devastated by Tyrone's condition, but she had to be positive for his sake. Even now, though, if he has an 'off' day she worries. 'It never leaves you, the fear that the slightest thing might start it up again,' explains Janet.

But Tyrone made good progress, and by early 1987, he was finishing his treatment, and was feeling well. Janet heard about Dreams Come True from the social worker at Great Ormond Street, who had arranged with Margaret to take several patients on a trip to Holland. Janet was longing for a break, and so she asked whether Tyrone might be included on a trip.

Within a few days, Margaret had telephoned Janet. They talked about what Tyrone liked best, was there a pop star he would like to meet? Janet replied the only thing he really loved was Thomas The Tank Engine. Would he like a ride then in a steam train, Margaret wanted to know.

Two weeks later, the telephone rang, and it was Margaret. 'I've arranged it all,' she said. 'Tyrone can come down to Sussex and see a train just like Thomas on the Bluebell Railway.' Janet was flabbergasted and Tyrone jumped up and down with joy. He was thrilled to bits just at the thought of seeing his favourite train.

On 2 April 1987, Janet and Tyrone took the train to Haywards Heath, where Margaret collected them from the station. Neither mother nor son had slept the night before, both were so excited at the idea of this day out. Janet was also so relieved that Tyrone was well enough to make it. They were joined by Sharon and Neil Minor from Warwickshire, whose little girl Theresa, who had cancer, was also a great fan of Thomas.

At the Bluebell Railway, the staff had arranged for them all to have a tasty lunch. They were joined by former Beatle Ringo Starr, the narrator and presenter of all the Thomas The Tank Engine shows and tapes. Ringo had bought the children presents, and Tyrone was given a Thomas train set. Ringo and Tyrone sat on the floor and played with it, and within minutes, the normally reserved little boy was clambering all over Ringo.

Later they went for a ride on the train, which was filled

with Thomas toys, and Ringo told stories which made everyone laugh and laugh. After some tea, and more presents of T-shirts, badges, books, posters and other Thomas goodies, everyone left for the day. Tyrone could not sleep that night either, he was so pleased with everything he had seen, with Ringo, with the people at the Bluebell Railway, and with Margaret. 'It was just the most marvellous tonic for everyone,' remembers Janet. 'Tyrone will never forget it, and neither will I. I'll never be able to thank Margaret enough for that day, and whatever happens, I will cherish the memory of it.'

Tyrone has been off his treatment for 12 months now, and he is fit and healthy, and at school. Whenever he feels a little low, he pulls out the photos of his day on the Bluebell Railway, and in next to no time, he is a happy, laughing child again.

Having had such a success at Santa World, Margaret decided that a trip to Legoland in Denmark would be a great idea. Set in the middle of the Danish countryside, Legoland has all the toys in the world ... a child's paradise. There have been trips to Holland too, and to Norway, and just about anywhere else a child might like to go.

But perhaps Margaret's trip of trips was in 1987, when she took 20 children, and their parents, on the *QE2* from Southampton to Cherbourg, and sent them on from there to Paris for three days, where they returned to London on the Orient Express.

The staff of Cunard's flagship could not have been kinder. For Rebecca Watkins, who had come through painful chemotherapy for leukaemia, it was an 18th birthday present never to be forgotten. By the time everyone was seated for lunch, the ship was steaming through the English Channel. The waiters appeared with a cake, and candles, and a resounding chorus of 'Happy Birthday To You'. And Rebecca was even more delighted when the Captain gave her an engraved silver plate as a present from the whole crew.

'We like to do what we can for young people like Rebecca, and it is an honour for the *QE2* to host a party like this. These children show the sort of courage we can only imagine,' said Captain Alan Bennell.

The day was filled with all sorts of treats. There was a variety show, with singing and dancing, and each child received a *QE2* T-shirt and teddy bear mascot.

There was a trip to the bridge for several youngsters, with Captain Bennell acting as tour guide. All the radars and gizmos, lots of bleeping sounds and clicking of the automatic navigational equipment, and even a chance to steer.

Sonia Hammersley, a pretty 18-year-old from Newcastle upon Tyne, with a serious leg tumour, was on board with her new husband Stephen Bell. Their romance had blossomed throughout Sonia's illness, and during the long painful months of hospitalisation, Stephen had sat by her side. This was to be their special moment; a blessing, performed by the priest who had married them only a few days earlier, on board the greatest ocean liner in the world. Under a clear blue sky, with the sea around them, and the bride dressed in the magnificent lace and silk dress she had worn on her wedding day, Sonia's and Stephen's union was blessed.

5

The Walk of Life . . . The Heart-Breakers

Some children suffer so much from their illnesses that it is impossible not to wonder why anyone so innocent or blameless as a young child ever has to go through such torture. Sometimes, when a very sick child dies, it is hard not to see their passing as a welcome release. Many terminally ill children achieve a serenity and inner peace before their deaths, and the wisdom and the strength they attain is frequently an invaluable crutch to their parents in the time of grief. Margaret believes that the children who die are destined for a better place. But while they live, their short lives enrich the lives of all of those who come into contact with them.

Cystic fibrosis is a genetic disorder which mainly affects young children, and stops the pancreas producing the necessary enzymes to digest food. Instead, the pancreas, an important organ in the digestive system, produces an excess of salt. The salt makes the body's secretions thicker than they should be. The salts work their way round the system in the blood. The salts in the lungs make the mucus thicker and stickier, and therefore it is harder to cough up. The results are two-fold. The chest becomes congested with mucus, and the patient becomes more susceptible to repeated infection. The lungs become fibrous, and the walls of the lungs break down into cysts, making it even harder for the oxygen to get from the lungs into the blood stream. Ultimately, the sufferer's chest becomes so congested, and the lungs so fibrous and holed with cysts, that breathing is impossible, and heart failure unavoidable. The treatment is constant, and children with cystic fibrosis spend a great deal of their time in hospital on extensive medication.

Charlene Philips from Coed Eva in South Wales was born with cystic fibrosis. At the local hospital, it was a matter of course to run tests on newly born babies, and at six weeks, doctors told Frank and Tricia Philips that their child had this genetic disorder for which there is no cure. But Charlene was a healthy-looking cheerful baby, and the Philips could not imagine what cystic fibrosis meant, as the child was feeding and growing normally.

At six months, the Philips had the first inkling of what to expect. A serious infection laid Charlene low, and she was rushed into hospital for treatment. She was very poorly, and it took her several days to recover. But cystic fibrosis is a progressive illness, and while Charlene grew into a chubby toddler, her parents found it hard to believe she would become seriously ill later.

Charlene was nearly three when her lungs burst. She had been less and less well. A pneumothorax, a cyst on the outside of her lungs caused by her disease, had opened, filling the chest cavity with air and causing her lungs to collapse. It nearly killed her, and for two months Charlene lay fighting for life in hospital, with drips in her tiny arms. Tricia hardly left her bedside, and Christopher, her brother, was yet another brother to feel neglected because of the attention devoted to a sick child.

Charlene was a cheerful little girl though, in spite of the treatment. She giggled with her parents and brother, and had a room full of cuddly toys. The treatment was severe, however. The intravenous antibiotics, to stave off infections, had to be administered daily, and as the disease progressed, the child became thinner and thinner, making it even harder to find a vein. Tricia remembers it all: 'It's just horrific, the child's arms were like a drug addict's. You have to keep on rebedding the needle, to get the drugs into them, but Charlene's arms were so thin it became more and more painful.'

Charlene took 32 tablets every day, not only to stimulate digestion, but to ease the discomfort of the congested chest. Tricia learned how to give her daughter the intravenous drugs at home, so that she would be able to spend as much time as possible with her family. As it was, Charlene spent about four months of each year in a hospital bed: three weeks there, maybe four at home, and then back to hospital again for more antibiotics. The whole houshold revolved around her. There was physiotherapy three times a day, to make the system work, and the family was ready, at the drop of a hat, to rally round if there was a crisis.

It was a slow existence for Charlene. She did not manage to go to school, because she was poorly so much of the time. Instead friends would come to the house, and she was a popular child with a lovely smile. Tricia and Frank tried to ignore the fact that she might not grow up, and just enjoyed each and every day they had with her. It was on a peaceful day at home that Tricia read in a magazine about Margaret and Dreams Come True. 'I remember reading the article,' Tricia says, 'and thinking, why do all these children get so many treats; why not my little girl? She's been through so much, she would love to have something special happen.'

With that, Tricia sat down and wrote to Margaret, telling her Charlene's story, and asking for help. Margaret phoned by return. Of course she would try to fulfil Charlene's dream. What, more than anything else, would she like? Charlene loved the Princess of Wales, and had a book of the Royal Wedding. More than anything, she would like a beautiful dress, just like those Diana's bridesmaids wore.

Margaret telephoned Elizabeth and David Emmanuel, who had designed and made the dress for that fairytale wedding, and explained Charlene's wish. They agreed at once to make her a dress, and Charlene sent them a drawing of what she would like. It was late March 1987 when Margaret telephoned them to say that everything was underway for the visit. The Philips were to travel up to London and meet the Emmanuels at the Waldorf Hotel. In addition, they would be part of a film being made for TVS, about Dreams Come True. The whole family was thrilled with the idea, and on 9 April, they piled into the family car, and headed for London.

But it was touch and go that they made it to London at all, for ten days before the trip, Charlene had been rushed back into hospital with a severe chest infection. The doctors had filled her up with massive doses of antibiotics to make her well enough for the journey.

The next day the Philips family arrived at the Waldorf to be greeted by Margaret and the film crew. They all had lunch together, and then moved upstairs to a suite set aside for the day. Charlene had to have a rest, she was tired by the sheer excitement of it all, and several coughing fits racked her tiny body. But the appearance of Elizabeth Emmanuel, bearing the most beautiful dress she had ever seen, soon perked her up. Everyone was sent into the lounge to wait, and Charlene was left in the hands of Elizabeth and David to get ready. The Emmanuels have a daughter of a similar age, and were used to helping little girls prepare for parties. They took the dress out of the cover, and Charlene gasped with pleasure. Made from silk and lace, the dress had hand-sewn rosebuds and pearls, and there was a matching hair-bow and tiny clutch bag filled with little sachets of perfume and pot-pourri. Taking each of them by the hand, Charlene made her entrance, and everyone was speechless. She looked gorgeous and just like a princess. 'We often talk about the day when I'll escort Charlene down the aisle, and we know it may never happen,' said Frank, 'but to see her walk in looking so beautiful, well, that's worth a million pounds of any man's money.'

The Emmanuels were visibly moved by Charlene's obvious delight. 'I think she liked it, I hope she did. We were certainly very happy to help any way we could. It's really moving to see how much the dress means to her. We're just happy that we could give Charlene something she really wanted,' said Elizabeth. 'Her mother told us what she'd been through, and we can't really imagine what it's like, because our children, thank God, are healthy. It's meant a lot to us to be here today, it's a privilege to meet a child like Charlene, she's very special,' David added.

Charlene's day was not yet over. Amid the laughter, there was a knock on the door. Charlene opened it – and there was her very favourite television personality, comedian Lenny Henry, beaming from ear to ear. 'I've come to take you to tea,' he announced. 'What a dress, Charlene, you look magnificent, I'll be so proud.' Then Lenny said as an afterthought: 'The Emmanuels never made me a dress. I demand some trousers!' With much hilarity, the party made their way to the restaurant for afternoon tea, where smiles remained the order of the day for several hours. 'It's great to be asked to do things like this,' said Lenny later. 'These kids go through so much, and if I can bring them some laughter, that's great. And the look on her face was fantastic, wasn't it?'

It took two weeks for Charlene to come down from the high caused by her trip to London. She put her dress on numerous times for neighbours and visitors to admire, and it hung on her bedroom door, a constant reminder of her day out. But her good health did not last, and by mid-June, Charlene was back in hospital. The infection in her chest had returned, and she was very poorly indeed. She had no more veins left, and the doctors felt she was too ill to put in a Hickman's catheter, which would have been placed in her chest to avoid having to use the veins at all to administer the drugs. In addition, Charlene was exhausted from trying to breathe. Her chest was full of hard mucus, and for ten days, the doctors tried to reduce the infection chemically. It did not work, and by now Charlene was becoming frightened because she could not breathe properly – even the ventilator did not help much any longer.

Tricia wrote to the Emmanuels, telling them how weak Charlene was. Within a couple of days, a package arrived containing a heart-shaped pillow, beautifully embroidered with rosebuds and pearls to match the dress. Charlene was enraptured and placed it by her bed. But she was now so ill that she asked for 'a man from God' to see her, and Tricia asked the Methodist minister attached to the hospital to talk with Charlene. The Philips were not religious people, but Charlene was convinced that she was going to heaven. The minister sat with her for three days, after which she was far more peaceful.

The doctors decided finally, and after much persuasion from Tricia and Frank, to remove the mucus under anaesthetic. They gave Charlene a 50/50 chance of pulling through, as she was so ill. She was in the theatre for nearly two hours, and her parents sat with the minister in the hospital chapel, praying for her life. They willed Charlene back to them, and she did regain consciousness from the anaesthetic.

Frank and Tricia were with their daughter in the recovery room, holding her in their arms, when she died on 7 July 1987. She was buried as she would have wished, wearing the dress, slippers and hair-bow, holding the little bag and with her head resting on the heart-shaped pillow. Frank and Tricia cherish the memory of their day in London, and remember Charlene laughing as she was on that day. 'Words can't express the affection and gratitude we feel to Margaret for giving us that memory.'

Robert Campbell first became ill when he was only eight and a half years old. His legs had started to ache, he was very pale, his throat was sore, and he was generally tired and run down. His mother, Jackie, knew the warning signs all too well, and she rushed him to her GP. She wanted Robert to have a blood test. It was 28 October 1974, and she had a whole weekend to wait for the results.

On Monday morning, the doctor telephoned. Something was very wrong with Robert, she told Jackie, and he was to keep away from other children to avoid infection. She advised them to take him up to London to Great Ormond Street Hospital, for further tests. Within half an hour, the Campbells were on their way to London from Haywards Heath. It did not take long for the specialists to confirm what Jackie already suspected. Robert had leukaemia, they told her and her husband Neil. Jackie and Neil were numbed and they had a terrible sinking feeling in their stomachs as they exchanged looks. They feared the worst with good cause. Jackie had lost her first husband from leukaemia; he had died six weeks after the disease was diagnosed. She was devastated, but made the decision there and then that if her son was likely to die, he would not lose courage by knowing that he too had leukaemia.

They kept Robert in Great Ormond Street for ten days, and Jackie moved in. Although the chemotherapy made him very sick, and the radiotherapy made his hair fall out, he took the treatment well, and within a matter of months, was back at school. He remained well, and a year later, he went to the junior school nearby at Hurstpierpoint. Most of the boys were boarders, but because Robert had been so ill, he could attend on a daily basis, so that blood tests and treatment could continue. Jackie remembers spoiling him rotten, overcompensating for his illness and for the treatment, which continued until he was 12. His little sister Maria, 20 months his junior, was rather a tomboy at the time and often played up. It was not until years later that she told her parents that she thought that they did not love her as much as Robert, and she was difficult because she craved some of the attention they bestowed so readily on him.

Robert's hair had grown back curly, and he was well enough to thoroughly enjoy school. He was a bright boy, and for nearly two years he thrived. He was 14, and had just passed his common entrance to the senior school. But after he had taken part in a 60-mile walk, the Levers Challenge, he started to feel unwell and thoroughly exhausted. He did not complain but was very listless. Jackie recognised the warning signs, and took him for a bone marrow test.

The leukaemia was back, and Robert was treated with stronger dosages of chemotherapy and radiotherapy. He hated it, and felt ill afterwards. He lost his hair again, and at 14, this was very hard for him to handle. But he was courageous and had immense spirit. For three years Robert stayed on the treatment, yet managed to pass eight O levels. It was in the second year of his A level studies that the doctors attempted a bone marrow transplant. Robert had not been feeling too well recently, but unfortunately none of his close relations' marrow matched his. He planned a trip to the Bahamas to stay with a school friend, and as Jackie and Neil saw him off at the airport, they knew that when he returned, he would have to undergo more treatment. Robert was 17, and a charming and gentle young man. When he returned from his holiday, Jackie and Neil decided it was time to tell him the truth about his illness. Robert was terribly upset, but thanked them for not telling him sooner. At least now he could cope, and would take the treatment in his stride. He learned to drive that summer, and passed his test only six weeks after starting lessons.

Robert decided to pursue a career in agriculture, and after taking his A levels, he set off for Plumpton Agricultural College. Meanwhile he had had a terrific 18th birthday party, as Jackie felt she really had something special to celebrate. 'I thought we were on borrowed time. I never thought that Robert would live to be 18. We were just so proud of him.'

The first two years at college were great fun, and Robert was a model student. That summer, Robert drove out to Barcelona to join a girlfriend who was working there, and stayed for six weeks. Jackie had had to have a hysterectomy, and ten days after she came out of hospital, Robert returned from Spain. Her heart sank when she saw him. She could sense that he was ill again, and a blood test the next day confirmed the bad news. The leukaemia had returned. Not only that, within days Robert had a serious infection, and this combined with the effects of more chemotherapy and radiotherapy made him very poorly indeed. He nearly died during that period, falling into a coma, and spent a lengthy period in the Intensive Therapy Unit. Jackie and Neil were distraught. Robert was bleeding badly inside, and they did not know if he would pull through. Jackie kept playing his favourite record, the Dire Straits song 'The Walk Of Life', over and over again to him. Eventually, Robert regained consciousness. He was very weak indeed, but was well enough to come home for Christmas.

Tragedy struck on 9 January 1987, when Neil Campbell suddenly died. Robert was much stronger now, and became a tower of strength to the family, helping everyone to rally around. The family had to carry on, and Robert's 21st birthday was a great excuse to lift the depression caused by Neil's tragic death. Jackie decided to splash out, and give Robert something he would always remember. Robert was car-mad, and she wondered how she could arrange for him to meet racing driver Nigel Mansell. As Margaret only lived up the road, Jackie thought she would pay her a visit. It was March 1987, and as she sat in Margaret's office, she noticed that there was a gold disc on the wall. She told Margaret Robert's story, and asked if she could possibly get hold of the gold disc of 'The Walk Of Life'. 'I'll see what I can do,' promised Margaret.

Several weeks later, Margaret rang Jackie in great excitement. 'I've got it for you,' she said. 'What?' asked Jackie. 'The disc!' Robert was absolutely overjoyed, and on his 21st birthday, he showed it to all his friends and family. Margaret had not forgotten that Robert wanted to meet Nigel Mansell, and the next weekend the Campbells travelled to Silverstone Race Track to speak with Nigel, who signed Robert's car with a flourish.

A couple of weeks went by, and Margaret telephoned Jackie again. Mark Knopfler, the lead singer with Dire Straits, had heard about Robert, and would like to meet him. The Campbells travelled up to the recording studios in London, and Mark re-presented Robert with the platinum disc. It was another great day, and Robert was the centre of attention. The band wanted to know all about him, his treatment, illness, his trips abroad and his day with Nigel Mansell.

At the Dreams Come True Ball at the Grosvenor Hotel that November, a happy-looking Robert was a key member of the festivities; he and his girlfriend Lucy danced the night away with a multitude of celebrities. These treats kept Robert going for some time, and that Christmas the family celebrated in style. It was a difficult time as it was the first Christmas without Neil, but everyone was in good spirits. At the end of January, Robert went in for another blood count. The doctors were worried, and decided to test his bone marrow.

The leukaemia was back, but now all the punch had gone out of Robert. He had been through so much traumatic treatment, over and over again, and for what? Jackie tried to make him fight, but he was just too tired. This time, she knew he would not make it.

'The last year of Robert's life couldn't have been better if he'd sat down and planned it himself,' said Jackie. 'He did everything he'd dreamed of, thanks to Margaret, and I'll never forget it.' Robert died on 23 March 1988; the song that had meant so much to him, 'The Walk Of Life', was played as a tribute at his funeral.

Belinda Catt from Tonbridge in Kent was another very

special child. At 14, she was in Penbury Hospital, dying from a painful stomach cancer which had not responded to treatment. Her mother, Sally, wanted only to bring a little happiness to her daughter before the inevitable happened.

Belinda was a huge fan of the pop group Madness, and was particularly keen on the lead singer, Suggs. She listened to their tapes on her personal cassette player in hospital, but as she became weaker, she could not tolerate any company at all. Margaret heard about Belinda through the local paper, and decided to pay her a visit. Belinda was very upset, and kept saying the only person she wanted to meet was Suggs. Margaret left and launched into action. She would make sure that Belinda did not die before her dream was fulfilled. After several phone calls to Suggs's agent, the visit was clinched.

The next week, Margaret travelled down to Tonbridge. Belinda was feeling particularly poorly and extremely depressed. Margaret popped her head into the small room and said hallo. 'I don't want to see anyone,' pleaded Belinda. 'But I've got someone special here to see you, Belinda darling,' said Margaret. In tears Belinda turned onto her side and fell asleep. The surprise visitor crept in, and sat on the edge of her bed. Margaret tried again: 'Belinda darling, please wake up I've got someone you really want to meet.'

'Hallo Belinda, how are you?' said Suggs. 'I've been really looking forward to seeing you. I've got some presents for you.' Belinda's eyes flew open and she screamed. She flung herself at Suggs and would not let him go, weeping tears of delight. Margaret and Sally left the room; they were too choked to stay. Suggs held Belinda close and sat with her for over an hour, and when he left, the child was resting. She smiled at her mother, and seemed content. 'I don't mind now if I die, Mummy, now that I've met Suggs,' she said. Two days later, a letter arrived at the hospital for Belinda. It was from the singer, thanking her for letting him come and visit her; she was thrilled.

Belinda's small body was riddled with cancer, and she died several days later.

Christopher Johnson from Liverpool was only three when his parents discovered all was not well. Steph, his mother, had a baby in January 1985, and soon Christopher started to be sick. The GP thought it was jealousy, but Steph and Alan Johnson were concerned. The doctor recommended that they take Christopher to Arrow Park Hospital in Liverpool for some counselling, and it was the staff there who suggested that the child should have a brain scan at Walton Hospital.

Christopher was scanned in the morning, and the consultant looked at the results there and then. He told Steph and Alan that Christopher had a brain tumour, and that it was unlikely he would live many more years. The Johnsons were shocked into silence. Steph said later that she knew something was very wrong, but she had no idea it would be so serious. They were referred to Clatterbridge

Hospital on the Wirral, for treatment. Christopher had a medullary blastema, a tumour right on the brain stem, so it was impossible to remove it surgically. The specialist recommended that Christopher have radiotherapy to reduce the tumour in size. Christopher was under Dr Brian Cottier, whom Steph remembers was 'marvellous'. Christopher would call him Uncle Brian, and the senior radiographer Auntie Joyce. He was a very affectionate child with a delightful grin, and he became a favourite with all the staff.

By June, his treatment was over, and a scan in September revealed that the tumour had gone. The Johnsons were delighted, but in October, Christopher was unwell again. He had started to projectile vomit, and was very thin. A scan in early November revealed the worst. The tumour had returned, and with a vengeance. Christmas that year was a blur of treatment and hospitals, sickness and despair.

Steph saw Margaret on TV-AM and contacted her. She mentioned that Christopher had lots of favourite things, but the absolute tops were the group Five Star, Thomas The Tank Engine, flashing police cars and Cilla Black. Soon a package arrived from Five Star, containing cassettes, T-shirts, badges, and a very sweet letter. Margaret also put Steph in touch with Mike McCartney, the brother of Beatle Paul, who got some signed Thomas the Tank Engine cassettes and books from the show's presenter, Ringo Starr.

Then the Johnsons were all invited to the pantomime at

Liverpool's Empire Theatre, where Cilla Black was playing Aladdin. A police car with every light blazing collected them, and Christopher was so excited. They sped through the Mersey Tunnel, and the little boy sat on his mother's lap, entranced. The policemen had even loaned him a helmet, from which he would not be parted. At the theatre Cilla appeared and went straight up to Christopher and gave him a warm hug, and asked him if he knew who she was. 'You're Cilla Black,' he replied.

'No I'm not, I'm Aladdin,' she joked.

'Oh dear,' said the giggling three-year-old. 'I am a Mr Forgetful!' Then Christopher could hardly contain himself when up through the trap-door in the middle of the stage popped Mike McCartney carrying a replica police pedal car and a small helmet. The Johnsons had a great time with the cast of *Aladdin*. It was to be one of the last happy outings for the family, for after Christopher's fourth birthday in April, he went rapidly downhill.

Christopher died on 13 May. But some good at least has arisen from his death, for Steph and Alan Johnson, inspired by Margaret's work, have started the Christpher Johnson Fund in memory of their son, to help seriously ill children.

Jason Britton never weighed more than three and a half stone, or grew above four feet in height, but he had the personality and courage of a giant. Jason, like so many of the children Dreams Come True helps, was born with cystic fibrosis, and spent long periods of his life in hospital.

He was the third of four children, and until he was seven, he was a bouncy, lively and athletic boy. Nobody could tell he had a terminal illness, and yet from the age of three months, Jason had been plagued with various problems. He had had mumps when he was two, and at four he had his first serious lung infection. But it was not until he was seven years old that he started the classic, chesty cystic cough, and from that time on, he did not grow.

To avoid having intravenous antibiotics in hospital Jason's mother, Marilyn, opted to treat him at home. Jason would inhale his antibiotics through an aerosol, and it would take him some twenty minutes each day to take in the necessary amount. He needed physiotherapy three times a day, especially in the morning before school. It was very time-consuming, but the family felt it was better than having him constantly hospitalised.

In fact Jason avoided hospital altogether until 1981, when his lung collapsed when he was aged 12. He was very ill indeed, and three months later, the lung collapsed again. The Brittons were beside themselves, but Jason was a real fighter, and he was back home within a few weeks. It was another three and a half years before he had to go back to hospital, but with each visit the treatment would take longer and longer, and the drugs had to be even stronger. He had naturally developed a tolerance to them, and they were not as effective as before.

Throughout that time, Jason continued to attend school, and was a very popular boy. He would always make fun of himself. If there was a knobbly knees competition, Jason would say he was sure to win it. The girls in the senior school would cuddle him and make a fuss of him because he was so tiny, which he loved. Marilyn remembers taking Jason with her to the local garage to fill her car up with petrol. He was nearly 17 at the time, but because he was so small, looked only seven or eight. The garage owner rapped on the window, most perplexed. The Brittons laughed and pointed out that it was not a child playing with a dangerous liquid.

As soon as Jason passed his driving test, he started to look for his own car. He made some money by selling products over the telephone from home, and had won several selling awards. He finally found a Suzuki automatic and had it converted. It had to be adapted so that both Jason and his mother could drive it. He adored that car and it tickled him to see people's faces as he drove up to shops or garages, when they clearly imagined that the young man behind the wheel was a juvenile joy-rider. He always laughed at this sort of thing and never took offence. Jason's sense of humour was his greatest asset. When he was selling products over the telephone, he would joke with clients about the oxygen that he had to take as he talked to them. When his body could not keep up with his active mind, Jason played the organ, or took photographs. He rigged up a darkroom at home, and was commissioned to photograph a couple of weddings. He tried never to let himself become depressed, and dutifully took his treatment.

Margaret had arranged for a close friend of his, Louise Jones, to meet singer Nick Hayward. Louise had met Nick at his studio and he took her to dinner; from that moment they were firm friends. Nick would telephone her in hospital to see how she was, and even invited Louise to his wedding much to her delight. Louise died while Nick was on honeymoon, and a saddened Nick flew back to attend her funeral.

Jason loved to sit on Louise's hospital bed, and whenever Nick telephoned, Jason would laugh and make Louise turn towards him, so he could watch her face. She repaid his thoughtfulness by telling Margaret about him. Margaret discovered that Jason loved the old Pinewood Studios black and white films, and the comedies with Norman Wisdom and Sid James. It was Norman Wisdom he wanted to meet.

In January 1983 the Brittons made their way to Oxford to see the pantomime *Robinson Crusoe*. Norman Wisdom was starring in it, and he was delighted to meet Jason. They laughed and laughed about being small, and compared notes on amusing incidents caused by their size. For months afterwards, Jason played the tapes he had collected, and retold the jokes Norman Wisdom had cracked.

Jason carried on, but towards Christmas 1985, he started to go downhill fast. Marilyn remembers that the week before he died, Jason watched a film on television about a girl with cystic fibrosis, and was deeply moved by it. 'Poor girl,' he kept saying, 'they haven't even given her oxygen.' He simply did not realise that he was equally ill.

On 12 December, Jason picked out his summer wardrobe from a catalogue, and sent his cheque off. He was always looking forward to things. He had just received a new electric wheelchair, and had fixed his oxygen bottle to the back, for ease of access. And he was busy making jam to sell. Jason never talked about death, and towards the end, when he was so ill, it must have crossed his mind. He told his mother, who was his constant companion, that he wanted to die in her arms. 'Two days before he died, he asked me for Chinese food. He wanted chicken noodle soup. But he was just too ill to eat it. He said we could microwave it later,' says Marilyn.

On the Thursday, he asked for the doctor, but by Friday, he had obviously given up. 'I've had enough, Mum, I just don't know what to do. I can't stand this any longer, I just can't go on,' he told her. He died in Marilyn's arms in the early hours of 14 December 1985. Marilyn and Graham Britton still feel Jason around the house, and often laugh at things he might have found funny. But they can never watch Norman Wisdom's films without shedding a tear.

Little Pete loved lambs, Smurfs, and Boy George, but not necessarily in that order. He was the apple of his parents' eyes, and Julie and David Osborne doted on their only child. They were very worried when Peewee, as they called him, started to cry with pain in August 1984, and they rushed him straight to the doctor. The dignosis was constipation, and Peewee and his parents were sent away. But some hours later, he was still very distressed, and as she was putting him to bed Julie noticed that he had some bruising on his back, which seemed to be spreading round his sides. She gathered him up, and with David, rushed at once to her nearest hospital in Brighton.

The baby was admitted, and after running numerous tests, the doctors advised the Osbornes to take Pete straight to Great Ormond Street Hospital in London. They did not like the look of what they saw, and wanted him to have more tests. Two-year-old Pete had cancer in his stomach, and there were secondaries all over his tiny body. He had fluid on his chest, and first of all this had to be drained off, to allow him to breathe easily. 'He was very brave,' remembers Julie. 'They didn't want to give him an anaesthetic, for fear of losing him. Pete cried because it hurt, but he was very good and lay still.'

For eight months, Little Pete had chemotherapy, and some surgery. The oncologist took away 95% of the tumour, but it was so widespread, there was little hope of controlling it. Peewee's hair fell out, and his parents told him he was just like a smurf. He was sent home to Brighton, and Julie slept by his side, both in and out of hospital. Julie read about Margaret in a magazine, and decided to see if she could arrange a treat to cheer up her brave little boy. Margaret was delighted to help, and arranged for Boy George's double to come to the hospital to see Peewee. Little Pete was thrilled, and giggled when he was allowed to tug on the famous braids. Some weeks later, Margaret arranged for a day on a farm, and Little Pete was delighted with the lambs and chickens, ponies and calves.

But Pete really was not getting any better, and the staff at the hospital were simply maintaining him on morphine. He loved his specialist, Dr Gillian Cree, and would often hug her and sit on her knee, and he adored Sister Sharpe, and would pester her to let him look at her photograph album of all the children she had looked after. When he played with the other children on the ward, Pete always wanted to give them his toys. Neighbours raised the money to send the Osbornes to Disneyland in America. For the first three days, they had a wonderful time, saw the sights, and lapped up the American way of life. But on the fourth day, Peewee was very poorly. He could not move, and Julie knew instinctively that they were losing him. On the fifth day of their trip, they flew back to England, and Peewee was rushed straight to hospital. For two more weeks, the brave boy struggled for life but on 20 June 1985 Little Pete gave up his tough battle.

Richard and Suzie Lowe, and their children Andrea and Paul, had been living in Pretoria in South Africa for several years, and were preparing for seven weeks leave. They regarded it as a recce, to see if they might like to move back to England permanently. But whatever happened, as it was Christmas 1984, they planned to have a jolly festive season.

A week or so before they were due to leave, Paul began

2

4

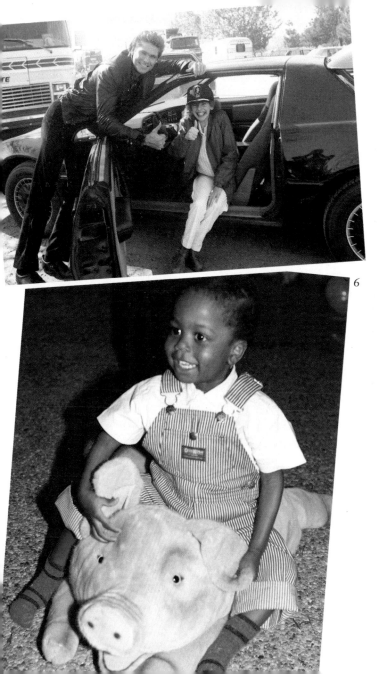

6

7

8

10

11

12

13

14

16

17

18

22

2

23

25

26

27

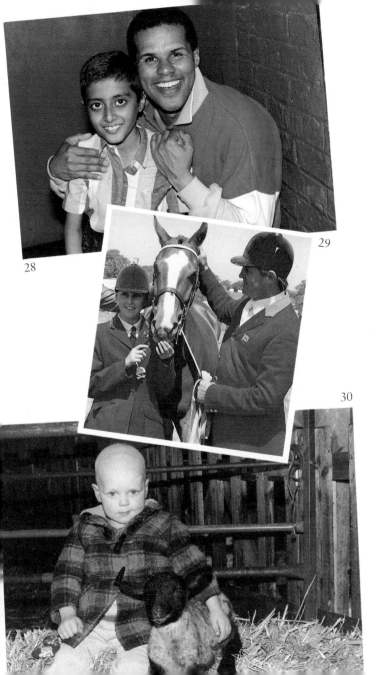

28

29

30

34

33

35

Margaret

36

to feel unwell. The ten-year-old was off his food, and after an examination, the doctor diagnosed glandular fever, and perhaps some anaemia too. There was no abnormality, he said, and Paul would certainly be well enough to fly. A holiday would do him good. Once in England they drove up to St Helens in Lancashire, where they would stay with Suzie's mother. Paul was very listless and felt exhausted all the time. He lay on the sofa, looking pale and drawn. Suzie, a former nurse, was becoming increasingly anxious, and was keen to get a second opinion.

The local GP seconded the opinion of his South African colleague. Glandular fever, he said, and accused Suzie of being an over-anxious mother. The next day, Suzie took Paul back and asked to see another doctor. Dr Robert Sills saw them this time, and referred the child at once to Whiston Hospital near Liverpool for tests. Suzie, by this time, was convinced she knew what was wrong with Paul. The consultants at Whiston confirmed her fears. 'It's almost certainly leukaemia,' they said. Paul was moved to Alder Hey Children's Hospital in Liverpool where he was diagnosed as having acute myloid leukaemia, a particularly severe form of the cancer. It is rare, and not very much is known about it, except the leukaemic infiltrations invade the spleen, the liver and the lymph glands, and most of the major organs in the body. Paul had to endure chemotherapy and radiotherapy. He would spend the first week in hospital to stabilise his blood levels, and then come home. But after three or four days, he would be back in hospital with an infection. It would take two weeks for that to clear up, and then he would be home again, feeling well for a week, before having to go back for more treatment.

Paul and Suzie were very close to each other, even before the onset of his illness, and now she was at his side around the clock. Paul pulled through, and by July, he was much better. Everyone was pleased, and for the next eight months, Paul rebuilt his strength and his life. The family had been forced to stay in England now. Andrea, Paul's older sister, had started a new school and had found new friends. Richard had a new job. But for Paul it was lonely. Because of his illness he had failed to meet other children his age, and now that he was well, he missed their company.

In March 1986, Paul had a relapse. He was very depressed because he knew exactly what was in store. The thought of more treatment, of losing his hair and being sick, of no school and no friends, upset him enormously. This time, the doctors put a central line in, and threaded a catheter from the elbow through a vein, into the heart. Through this line, Paul took his stronger drugs, and while it was easier to administer them, it was harder to absorb them too. Paul was sicker than ever. More drugs were administered to combat the nausea, and these made him high as a kite. After the treatment was over, he picked up every infection, and spent six out of every eight weeks in hospital. The doctors monitored his heart, afraid that it would go into failure from all the drugs, but Paul survived, and through 1986 and into 1987, he was relatively well.

In May 1987, Paul felt ill again. His heart failed, and treatment had to stop. Suzie and Richard were scared that the leukaemia would return if their son stopped the chemotherapy, but it was either that or risk heart failure. In June, the leukaemia returned, with renewed strength. The doctors tried to keep Paul's spirits up by putting him on steroids which gave him a feeling of well-being, but they knew it was only a matter of time. By now, Paul was 13, and had missed out on so much. The nurses read to him, and made him laugh, but it was not enough. One evening, a nurse was sitting on the side of Paul's bed, and she asked him what he would like more than anything else in the world.

'To swim with some dolphins,' was his immediate reply. Paul loved big marine creatures, and had several books on whales, dolphins and sharks. The nurse knew exactly what to do, and within a few days, Margaret had gone into action. Paul was very poorly, and Margaret knew that there was no time to lose. She telephoned Brighton Aquarium, and the director agreed at once to prepare the dolphins for their special visitor. Margaret rang the hospital, and the telephone was wheeled to Paul's bedside. Margaret asked him if he would like to swim with some dolphins, and the boy's face lit up. Even though he was so ill, it cheered him up at once. The doctors agreed that Paul could go to Brighton.

But the day of the journey Paul was very ill, so in

preparation for the trip the staff topped him up with steroids, with blood to reverse the anaemia, and with platelets to help normal clotting, prevent bleeding and stop bruising. It was a disaster, for within minutes Paul had a severe reaction. He swelled up and was covered with a rash; his tongue and mouth were so enlarged that he could hardly breathe. Anti-histamines made the swelling reduce, and once that was under control, the Lowes were off to Brighton. It was January 1988, and a taxi met the train at the station, and whisked them off to the Ramada Renaissance Hotel in the centre of Brighton. Paul was thrilled with the hotel as it was brand new, and very luxurious. Because he was on steroids, he could eat anything and everything, and he did. Nothing was too much trouble for the hotel, and the word 'no' was never uttered.

Margaret arrived and joined them for tea. She whooshed into the room, cheerful and jolly, and the Lowes immediately took to her. There was much chat and laughter, and everyone had a pleasant evening. A nurse, Janet, had travelled with the family to Brighton to look after Paul, and Suzie and Richard were very grateful for her that evening. Paul was very ill, and only the diamorphine could make him feel better. He *had* to be well enough to swim the next day with the dolphins, and Paul was determined that he would fulfil his dream.

The following morning, Paul rallied round, much to everyone's delight. It had been such an effort for the youngster to get there, it would have been a shame to miss the real highlight. The family, with Margaret and the nurse, made their way to the dolphinarium, where Paul put on a wetsuit to keep warm. He was thrilled to see these friendly dophins swimming in the tank, but was amazed to find another surprise waiting for him by the steps to the pool. His very favourite pin-up and pop star, Samantha Fox, was waiting in her wetsuit to join him for a swim. He was over the moon, especially when she made sure he was the centre of attention by giving him a big hug and a kiss, and chatting with him as if she had known him all his life. Then in she jumped, and as is normal, the dolphins gave her lots of space to swim in, while they got used to her. But the dolphins seemed to sense that Paul was very weak, and a female dolphin swam very close by, as Paul got in. She stayed with him, allowing him to hold her fin, and gently swam around the pool. She nuzzled him, and kissed him, and Paul was in seventh heaven. After several minutes of swimming, Paul was tired, and it was time to go.

Back in St Helens, Paul started to deteriorate rapidly. It was now only a matter of time. Some friends arranged for Paul to have a ride in a Porsche car, and this cheered him up, as he had always admired these sleek German machines. But he was very very ill. He had a high temperature, and was on oxygen to help him breathe, and diamorphine to relieve the pain. He was exhausted and his heart was failing.

When he started to vomit blood, Paul asked his mother if he could go back to hospital. 'Are you sure?' she said.

'Yes, I want them to help me.' The doctors put three drips into his arms: platelets and saline in one, to stop the bleeding and keep the veins open, and diamorphine to control the pain, and maxilon to control the sickness. That was on Friday. On Sunday, he was asleep, but he was smiling. 'Paul, what are you smiling at ?' asked Suzie.

'I dreamed that Jesus and Grandad were here,' he said, 'and Grandad smiled at me, and said that Jesus had come for all the children, and me too.' Paul smiled again, and said, 'Goodbye Jesus, goodbye Grandad.' At five minutes to one, on 28 February 1988, Paul Lowe died in his parents' arms. The staff later said there was a feeling of peace passing over the ward at that moment. It was a mere two weeks since the female dophin had looked after him in the pool.

Matthew Halpin was only three years old when doctors diagnosed leukaemia. He had been very run down, and had broken out in an uncomfortable rash. His mother, Julie, had taken him to Newport Hospital in Gwent, while her husband Ernest looked after the other children, Belinda and Shaun, and baby Alex. Julie remembers all too well the anxious feelings: 'I just couldn't imagine that anything was seriously wrong with Matthew. He was such a happy and cheerful child, and so full of life, that we just thought it was another children's virus.' After he was examined, however, she was left in no doubt. Matthew would have to undergo chemotherapy and radiotherapy to combat the disease.

It could not have come at a worse time. The other children were all so young, and Julie really needed to be at home with them. But Matthew needed her even more, and so for several weeks, the family coped with Julie being away for three nights a week while Matthew's treatment continued. Like all the children undergoing the exhaustive course of drugs, he was very sick, and became quite depressed. But he did go into remission, and for some eight months, Matthew was able to come home and live a normal life.

But in February 1988, the leukaemia returned. By this time, his mother had become pregnant and was increasingly worried about her son. Matthew returned to hospital in Cardiff, and had another course of chemotherapy and radiotherapy. He slept a great deal, but would wake up at lunchtime, just in time for the BBC *One O'Clock News*. Matthew liked to watch newsreader Martyn Lewis, and would recognise his voice whenever he heard it. He would automatically wake up in time for the *News*. When he was at home, there were discussions about whose voice could be heard. Matthew always picked out his favourite newsreader's voice.

One of the nurses in the hospital suggested to Julie that she should drop a line to Margaret, to see if she could arrange for Matthew to meet his hero. Margaret rang the BBC press office as soon as she received the letter, and was told that Martyn Lewis would be delighted to meet Matthew. On 13 June 1988, the Halpins drove up to London to the BBC's Shepherd's Bush Studios. Ernest was in charge that day, and had brought Matthew, and his older brother and sister. Julie was very pregnant by now, and had decided to stay at home with her youngest child. Matthew was full of beans, and was fascinated by the control room, the videotape area, and the studio itself. Martyn Lewis could not have been kinder to the children, and played with them for an hour. Then he gave them a videotape of the day, a most prized posession, which the Halpins took back to Gwent with them.

Matthew went downhill rapidly. He started to bleed internally again, and his heart could not cope with the drugs. Matthew died seven days after he returned from London.

Hannah Gillard, at 11, was a tall and slender girl, with a magnificent head of hair. Long straight blonde locks hung almost to her waist. She loved to dance and swim, ride and run, and she lived life to the full. The summer term at her school in Barnstaple in Devon had been a busy one. There had been the usual exams, but Hannah had also taken part in a dance show. Towards the end of term, then, it was really no surprise that she was tired. Her mother Carol put this down to too much activity, and thought little about it. After term broke up, Hannah was still tired, and had lost her normally healthy appetite. Carol took her to the doctor for a blood test. He thought she might have leukaemia, and referred her to the local hospital in Barnstaple for a bone marrow test the following day.

The Walk of Life

It was Wednesday by now, and the day of Prince Andrew's and Sarah Ferguson's wedding. Carol can remember Hannah refusing to leave the house until she had seen what Fergie was wearing, unaware of the torment her mother was going through. For while Hannah did not really understand what leukaemia meant, her mother knew the implications of a bone marrow test. Satisfied that the new Duchess of York looked lovely, Hannah and Carol went off to hospital. The results showed that Hannah did not have leukaemia; the news was even worse for she had rhabdomyosarcoma. This is a cancer of the muscle tissue, which had spread into the bone marrow. The next day, she was to go to Bristol Children's Hospital, and by then, she was really quite ill. It had only taken four days, it seemed to Carol, for Hannah to deteriorate rapidly. She was very pale and extremely tired.

Carol turned to her church for support, and found her strong Christian faith a great comfort to her and to the rest of her family. Hannah was the youngest of three children, and it was to them that she looked now, hoping that they and their father would cope without her. Carol also joined CLIC, the Cancer and Leukaemia in Children Trust, set up by Bristol Children's Hospital to help the families of victims. They had a lovely Georgian house near the hospital, and the parents could stay there while their children had treatment. It was also an opportunity to meet and talk with others in the same situation, and to feel that one was not alone.

Hannah was so exhausted by now that she really did not notice much of what was happening around her. She was prepared for chemotherapy, and because she quickly developed a needle phobia, a Hickman's catheter was inserted surgically in her chest. Hannah was always a rather dramatic child, and very sensitive, and by the time the chemotherapy had started, she was feeling better, and was quite frightened. She worried about losing her hair, most of all, and was very depressed about it. Carol remembers brushing Hannah's magnificent long blonde hair and it coming away in handfuls. This was very distressing for both mother and daughter, and within three days, Hannah had lost the lot. There were child psychologists on the ward, and the staff were very experienced, and helped Hannah over this period. She responded well to the chemotherapy and radiotherapy, and by early September she was back in Devon. By the end of that month, she was taking part in the Barnstaple carnival, dressed as a cowgirl. That term, she managed quite a lot of school, and spent time with her friends and family. She went riding and between treatments, led a normal life.

Through October and November, she was well, but in mid-December Hannah had septicaemia, and was back in hospital for two weeks. Fortunately, she managed to be well enough to go to St Albans for Christmas to see Carol's brother and his family. She had lost a lot of weight, but she was picking up a bit. In January, Hannah started to be very sick again, and was vomiting. It was the beginning of the relapse, and on 18 January, she was back in Bristol Children's Hospital, wheelchair-bound. She never walked again after that time, she was just too weak. She had now lost even more weight, and in the two days after arriving at Bristol, she once again went downhill fast. The cancer had spread into her central nervous system. It was very upsetting. She could not speak, and just made odd noises. The ups and downs were taking their toll, and every fibre of Carol's being felt wrung out. The emotions were raw, but Hannah kept her going, for in spite of her terrible illness, she still managed to smile at everyone, and before her brain was affected, she had been able to tell jokes and sing.

A valve was inserted into Hannah's brain, to enable the chemotherapy to go straight into the central nervous system, and she began to improve. By 18 March 1987, she was well enough to be transferred back to Barnstaple Hospital. It was at this point that Margaret heard about Hannah, through the hospital. She wanted to give her a treat, and knew, because she was so ill, that it would have to be soon. At first she suggested that Hannah might like to join a trip to Amsterdam, but she was too ill. But there was to be a trip on the *QE2* to Cherbourg, on to Paris, and returning by the Orient Express. Maybe Hannah would be well enough for that? Carol was delighted. Not only would it be a fantastic experience, but it would give the whole family a goal, something to look forward to. She only told Hannah about the trip a few weeks before, but the 14-year-old was very excited, and thoroughly looking forward to it.

Hannah was well enough to travel to Southampton on 21 July 1987, and loved the whole thing. She had regained her speech, and was able to join in. The *QE2* laid on a delicious lunch, but Hannah was not able to eat it. The chemotherapy made her nauseous, and she was very tired. In fact Carol had brough a pillow with her, so that Hannah could just be lifted out of her wheelchair, to lie down wherever she was. After lunch, the *QE2* put on some entertainment for the youngsters, and gave them all T-shirts and cuddly toys. They also played some disco music, and Carol can remember Hannah, who had always loved to dance, smiling from ear to ear as she 'danced' in her buggy. In the coach on the way to Paris, Hannah took the microphone from the courier, and told jokes to everyone in the group. There was lots of laughter that day, and Hannah topped it all by singing to everyone.

She had made the very best of her trip, although she had almost certainly been feeling wretched. Afterwards, Hannah looked back on the trip as something very special, and enjoyed telling everyone about the *QE2* and the Orient Express. Ten days later, she celebrated her birthday on 31 July in Barnstaple Hospital. But Hannah was deteriorating fast, and there were periods of not being able to talk. She was sent back to Bristol, and a shunt was put in her head to relieve the vomiting. It worked, and she recovered. But a few days later, she started to vomit again, and this time the doctors told Carol that the cancer was now in the brain. Carol decided that as there was nothing more that could be done, she would bring Hannah back to her family for her last days. On 13 August 1987 Hannah died at home.

Sharon Collins, a stunning 22-year-old from Weston-super-Mare, was born with cystic fibrosis. Although on medication since birth, she had been able to have a normal childhood, attend the local school, and make lots of good friends. But by the time she was 12, Sharon's chest infections were becoming more severe, and the damage was more pronounced. Each infection meant a spell in hospital, with increased medication and physio-therapy to clear the chest. School became less regular, and with each absence, catching up was more and more difficult. But Sharon has always been an exceptionally bright girl, with a huge personality, and while treatment has been hard, and often very unpleasant, Sharon's good humour won the day. At the local hospital, she was always a favourite, with a laugh and a joke for everyone. At home, an only child, she was her mother's best friend.

As if Sharon did not have quite enough on her plate, a week before her seventeenth birthday, she noticed a lump in her neck, that kept on coming up, and going down. At the local hospital, the doctors recommended a biopsy. The results revealed cancer of the lymph glands, Hodgkin's Disease. Because of the cystic fibrosis, chemotherapy was out of the question because Sharon's system simply could not cope with the massive doses of drugs needed. The only answer was radiotherapy, which is uncomfortable and unpleasant. She burst into tears at the distressing news, but soon recovered her composure. 'Okay,' she said. 'Let's get on with it. I'm too young to die, and I don't want to be stuck in this hospital bed for ever.' The staff at Bristol Children's Hospital responded at once, and the treatment was completed within a few weeks. The cancer appeared to have gone.

But the treatment exacted a price, for a year later Sharon's lungs totally collapsed after a particularly severe chest infection, and there were fears that she might not recover. Even so, Heather recalls, Sharon's good looks wreaked havoc among the local boys. A boyfriend came to visit her and one day, when he appeared with a hangover, Sharon told him he looked dreadful, in fact even worse than she did, a conversation which greatly amused the staff.

She was cheerful but, she remembers, she was thoroughly fed up with it all. That is when she met Margaret, who was able to put a whole new complexion on things. Margaret was on one of her hospital visits, and Sharon was sitting in bed, looking very poorly. The meeting was brief, but memorable. Margaret simply wanted to know who Sharon's favourite star was, and would she like to meet him. The answers were prompt. David Bowie and yes. Several weeks went by, and Sharon became stronger. Then a phone call from Margaret moved the Collins family into top gear. 'It's fixed,' said Margaret. 'Come down to London and David Bowie will put you up in the Grosvenor House on Park Lane, and will look also after you for the day.' A fast excursion to the shops followed, new hair styles and new outfits were organised, and off they set for London.

The hotel was magnificent, and there were flowers in the room and fresh fruit and chocolates for them. Within a few minutes, Margaret had telephoned, to explain what would happen the next day. With many smiles, Sharon and her mother settled down for some dinner, and a good night's sleep. The following morning, the car arrived to take them to the film set where David was working. Margaret was alongside, her usual cheery self, and was enjoying the pleasure her two companions so obviously felt. 'There he is,' said Sharon suddenly. 'He's up there, on that crane.' Sure enough, David was in the basket of the crane, but was coming down to ground level. 'I could not believe he was there, I could hardly believe I was there,' says Sharon.

David jumped down from the crane and smiling happily, he walked straight up to Sharon, and gave her a kiss and a hug. 'I'm so sorry you've been kept waiting,' he said, 'but you look great, and I've really been looking forward to meeting you. Come on, I'm hungry, let's all get some lunch.' Off they trooped, and the time just sped by. David wanted to know all about Sharon's illness, and was amazed by what she had been through. He showered her with gifts, and they parted after a couple of hours, sad to bid each other farewell. 'He was so friendly,' said Sharon. 'It was like a fatherly talk, he was really unaffected, and so normal.'

Back in Weston-super-Mare, life carried on. Sharon

was thrilled with her London trip, signed photos adorned her walls, while Heather had struck up a warm friendship with Margaret. 'She's so comforting, she really sometimes seems like the only person who understands. She doesn't mind when we phone, she's always pleased to talk to us.'

Margaret became very fond of Sharon. Her admiration for the way with which she coped with life was boundless, and Margaret would ring every few weeks to see how Sharon was getting on. It was over a year later, when Sharon had just turned 20, that the bad news came. Sharon's neck was sore again, and the lump was back. Bristol Children's Hospital confirmed the worst. The cancer had returned, and once again, Sharon would have to have radiotherapy. Her comment was brief and succinct, and summed up her feelings perfectly: 'OH SHIT!'

Sharon had more radiotherapy, and in spite of the discomforts of treatment, endeavoured to remain cheerful. It was on one of Margaret's routine calls to Heather that she learned that Sharon was ill again. 'Well, we'll just have to give her something to look forward to,' announced Margaret. And within a few days, she was back on the line. Montreux was on the horizon and Sharon and Heather must come. It was precisely the tonic Sharon needed, and by departure day she was in good enough shape to travel. She had the time of her life, dancing with the pop stars and snuggling up to Paul Young, as well as going to picnics and parties. She chatted with Phil Collins, met Annie Lennox, danced with A-Ha, and felt happily overwhelmed by it all. Laughter rang around the hotel, and Sharon thoroughly enjoyed herself with the other kids.

Sharon returned to a normal life, and carried on enjoying herself until April 1988, when after she had been out with her pals at the local pub, and on the way home, her lungs started to haemorrhage. She lost a pint of blood through her mouth and nose in the street, and was rushed to hospital. Heather sat by her bedside. When Sharon woke up at five am, she was amazed to see her mother there. 'What are you doing here?' she asked. 'Go home to bed. I'm not going to die tonight.'

But the damage was very severe. Sharon's lungs had so many bleeding points that the haemoptysis, or chest bleeding, was almost impossible to staunch. She was put on two-hourly injections of diamorphine, a sophisticated form of heroin, and after a few weeks as Sharon was so weak, and there was so little the doctors could do, she was sent home to die. The ambulance drew up at the Collins's house in Weston-super-Mare, and Sharon was put into her own bed.

Three hours later, Heather heard her daughter get up. 'I'm going out to buy a hamster. I'm bored with being in the bedroom with nothing to amuse me,' explained Sharon. 'Flash' the hamster was brought home, and miraculously, a few days later the girl, who earlier that week had been given just two or three days to live, walked into her best friend's 21st birthday party.

However the seven weeks on diamorphine took their

toll. On top of everything else Sharon was now a drug addict. But she was not daunted. 'Cystic fibrosis didn't kill me, and neither did cancer. I'm damned if drugs will get me either,' she said. But the cold turkey, with its cramps and vomiting, was awful; nevertheless she succeeded.

Sharon Collins was in a wheelchair, and used methadone to control the pain. But the spirited young woman laughed at her illnesses, and enjoyed every second of her life. Her favourite person, apart from her mum, was Margaret. 'She's always there for me, she never forgets me, and I know that when I'm down, Margaret seems to just know, and finds something to cheer me up and keep me going.' Sharon died on 24 August 1988; she had bid her farewells, put her affairs in order, and, exhausted by the unrelenting pain, closed her eyes.

6

The Miracle Children

There have been children whose recoveries can only be called miracles. In the six years of Dreams Come True, Margaret has come across children who really should never have survived, but who have, against all the odds.

Four-year-old Kelly Hardman from Brighton had been unwell for some time, and her mother, Joy, decided to take her to see her local GP. There was some swelling, but the doctor simply thought Kelly had an upset stomach. Kelly went from bad to worse, and after six months of constantly asking the GP to refer her to hospital, and his refusal, telling Joy she was over-anxious, Joy took Kelly to the hospital herself. After an examination, the child was admitted for immediate surgery. They put her on a drip at once; it was one donated by Cancer Research. Joy remembers seeing the label on the side of the bottle, and panicking. 'It was all I could think of, that drip from Cancer Research, and I thought, Oh God, no, please don't let this be happening to me.'

The doctors operated at once, and removed a malignant tumour (which weighed seven pounds) from Kelly's kidney, and the kidney itself. Kelly now weighed just twenty pounds and was desperately ill. Seven days after her operation, she was discharged, but the following few months were a nightmare. Each Monday, Kelly would have chemotherapy, and for the next two days she would be sick. Radiation would follow and that also made her ill. It was a roundabout of sickness and pain for the little girl, and a time of terrible anguish for her mother.

A phone call from the social worker at the hospital put Joy Hardman in touch with Dreams Come True. Did she want to take Kelly to Switzerland, with the whole family, to convalesce? Joy thought it was a hoax. 'I'd never heard of Dreams Come True, and I thought, that's it, I've had enough, I can't take any more.'

She soon realised that it was for real. She met Margaret, whom she thought at first was overpowering, but whom she soon grew to like and respect. Brian Beaumont, of Swiss Holiday Caravans, was always willing to make one of his mobile homes available to the charity for the use of parents and recovering children, and it was to one of these that the Hardmans went. Margaret wanted the whole family to go. It would be an opportunity for them to rest, and for Kelly's older brother, Shane, who was seven at the time, to receive a little special attention.

'Most people don't realise the stress the whole family is under when you have a very sick child. We try to help the whole unit with holidays like this, to give them the courage to carry on. It's amazing how it helps,' points out Margaret.

Joy remembers: 'The scenery was breathtaking, and for the first time in months, we managed to laugh and enjoy ourselves, without spending every minute worrying about Kelly.'

After the trip, the Hardmans returned, and Kelly continued her treatment. Her greatest hero had always been puppeteer Keith Harris, and his duck Orville. One day, bright and early, Joy Hardman dressed the little girl in a beautiful red velvet dress, with a white collar, made by the wife of a policeman for whom Joy worked part-time, and took her on a trip to the Leisure Centre in nearby Crawley. Keith Harris was performing there, and between shows, he met Kelly who was quite overcome at meeting Orville. 'She was astonished, she didn't know whether to laugh or cry. Every emotion was written on that child's face,' says Joy. 'It was worth everything for that one moment.'

Kelly sang Orville's favourite song to him. 'Orville, I love you, please don't fly away' and Keith Harris promised that Orville would wave to her when he appeared on television the next morning; and to Kelly's delight Orville remembered. Joy is convinced that meeting the fluffy duck helped Kelly regain her health, as she was able to tell all her friends about it and forget totally about her treatment for a while.

It is now five years since Kelly was ill, and Margaret

has kept in touch with the family. Today Kelly is a plump healthy nine-year-old, who enjoys everything to the full.

Adam McQueen is another very special child. Seven years ago, when he was only four, his grandmother noticed that he was knocking his feet together when he walked. After a week, he was stumbling and falling over. The GP thought he was having problems with his bones, and referred him at once to an orthopaedic surgeon, who decided that Adam must have a trapped nerve in his spine, and sent him to a neurologist at Treliske Hospital. It was to take over a week, and the McQueens were more than worried. Geoffrey McQueen, a Chief Petty Officer in the Navy, contacted the Naval Hospital, and after several phone calls, Adam was seen the next day by the naval neurologist Mr Herring. It was the beginning of a nightmare for the whole family. The neurologist took one look at Adam, and ordered x-rays. He told Jenny and Geoffrey that their son had a growth which was either on the spine or the brain. They were to take Adam that very night to Freedom Fields Hospital in Plymouth, without delay.

'We could not believe that Adam had something seriously wrong with him. He'd never had a day's illness in his life, not even the usual childhood things like chicken pox or mumps. We were in shock,' said Jenny.

It took them till 10.30 that evening to reach Plymouth from Falmouth, Cornwall, and the hospital was imposing, and frightening in a Victorian way. 'I wondered what on earth was going to happen,' said Jenny.

The result of the brain scan the next day was bad. A tumour that was clearly malignant, the size of a five-pence piece, in Adam's middle brain. It was growing daily, and because it was in the mid-brain, it was affecting his every movement. By now, Adam looked as though he had had a stroke. The left side of his body was contorted, he could not walk, could hardly speak, and was in some pain from his twisted joints. The tumour was inoperable, and Adam's condition was deteriorating before their eyes. A ventricular shunt to relieve the pressure on the brain was put in under anaesthetic. The doctor shaved Adam's head, and because the shunt was on the outside, Jenny and Geoffrey were horrified when they saw their only child returned from theatre.

Their world was falling apart, but they had to be strong for Adam's sake. When Jenny told him what was wrong, he could not really understand. 'But there's nothing growing on me. I must be all right,' he said.

The next six months were spent at Adam's side, playing with him and keeping him occupied. The radiotherapy made the child sick, but in spite of everything, the McQueens remained courageous. They became closer as a family, spending more time together in the hospital than they had ever done at home. 'The ward became our home,' said Jenny. 'We became great friends with nurses and doctors, and the other people in a similar situation.'

After the radiotherapy ended, Adam's chances did not look good and there was nothing left to do but to send

the lad home to die. It was a painful and bleak few weeks
that followed. Jenny remembers that people would cross
the road rather than speak to her. Many of her so-called
friends simply could not cope with Jenny and her sick
child. Three weeks went by, and Jenny and Geoffrey, who
had unlimited compassionate leave from the Navy,
became more and more depressed. They did not know
where to turn. The Catholic priest who married them, and
the Methodist minister who christened Adam, were too
busy to call. Jenny, who had always believed strongly in
God, felt desolate. 'I had had so much trouble conceiving
and having Adam, that I had always thought he was a gift
from God,' she explained tearfully.

She noticed an advertisement in her local paper calling
people to attend a service held by an evangelical faith
healer, Brother John. It was to be held in the Seamen's
Mission in Falmouth, that very afternoon. Jenny's grandfather had founded that Mission, and so the McQueens
decided they had nothing to lose. They would go along,
even though it was pouring with rain. Jenny cried
throughout the beautiful service, and the congregation
prayed for Adam's recovery.

'As he was a gift from God, in my view, I felt it was
time for God to either take him to a better place, or give
him back to me. I couldn't bear the limbo.' The
McQueens came out of the Mission, feeling much
heartened. They had spoken with Brother John, and
found him enlightening and comforting. And now the sun
was shining brightly, a rainbow in the sky.

The weeks went by but still Adam could only lie on cushions on the floor to play with his toys. He could not walk, and Mr Mohan, the specialist, had said that Adam would probably never walk again. The children in the street played nearby, and the sound of laughter often filled the long lounge in the McQueen's house. But it was not Adam's laughter.

Six weeks after Adam had been sent home from hospital it was a rainy Saturday afternoon. Jenny had decided to make some tea and toasted tea cakes for them to eat while Geoffrey watched the rugby on television. Adam was on his cushions, at the far end of the room, quietly playing with his toys. When Jenny came back into the room, with her laden tray, she let out a terrific scream and dropped the lot. Adam had got up, and was walking towards her. It was a miracle in their eyes; they had never thought they would see their son walk again.

Months of rigorous physiotherapy followed, and it was a very different Adam who, 12 months after his discharge from hospital to die, walked into Mr Mohan's rooms at the Freedom Fields Hospital in Plymouth. A brain scan showed the tumour was reduced by two-thirds. A year later, it was the size of a pin-head. Three years on it disappeared altogether. The doctors could not believe nor explain it and did not know what to say.

Jenny started to raise money for cancer research, and it was on a cold winter's evening when she and the family attended a function to hand over a cheque. There were few people there, but amongst them was Jenny Eddy, the mother of Amanda, who had been on Margaret's first trip to Montreux. A friendship developed, and it soon transpired that Adam, more than anything else, wanted to meet the pop group Madness.

A few days later, Margaret telephoned Jenny McQueen to arrange for the whole family to have a few days in London, with a special treat for Adam in store. The McQueens listened to Madness's hit record 'Baggy Trousers' on the car cassette all the way to London, and Jenny knew it was going to be an exciting time for the lively seven-year-old.

They were to be at Madame Tussaud's Wax Works in London, for a conducted tour. Adam was over the moon at the thought of all the amazing figures in wax. They were taken up to the finishing room, and Adam was told that the wax figures of his favourite group were now ready, standing in the middle of the room, shrouded with a sheet.

It was for Adam to unveil them. 'They're really realistic,' said the little boy, filled with awe. Then the lead singer, Suggs, winked.

'Wax models can't wink, can they?' asked a perplexed Adam.

'No they can't,' chorused the group, as they came alive. It was a moving moment, with Adam's face filled with surprise and pleasure. In his excitement he was shifting about from foot to foot, hands in his pockets, and Suggs suggested that he might need to go to the toilet. Adam knew exactly what to say as since his illness, he had been a thin child, and his clothes were large on him. 'No, I just have baggy trousers!' The room filled with laughter. The group spent the whole morning with the McQueens talking about Adam's illness, and enjoying their company. It was a special day for everyone, and a tired but happy Adam left the wax-works, clutching a gold disc which had been presented to him by Suggs. But that was not the end of Madness and the McQueens. The group sent tickets to their next concert in Cornwall, and even took the family for dinner afterwards.

'Margaret made Adam happier than he'd ever been. Nobody has ever touched our lives in the way she has.' Jenny McQueen still spends time with Margaret whenever she can, fund-raising, attending functions given by the charity, and spreading the word.

Thirteen-year-old Carla Penta was crossing the busy A23 road when she had the accident. The first car threw her under a second car, and the second car threw her under a third car.

Her arms and legs, and her pelvis, were smashed, and for months she lay immobile in hospital, strung up to mimimise movement, and in considerable pain. Margaret read of Carla's terrifying accident in the local paper, and rang the hospital straight away. She spoke with the staff, and soon with Carla herself. Margaret realised how deeply depressed the child was, and resolved to make her happy.

Carla's one comfort in hospital was her personal stereo,

and she listened all day to the cassettes of pop singer Howard Jones. He was her idol, and she had masses of photographs of him and all his hit records. Margaret rang up Howard Jones's management as soon as she got home, much saddened by her visit with Carla. Within a few hours, Howard's manager rang Margaret, and explained that Howard was about to leave on a world tour. Howard wrote Carla a long letter, enclosing a cassette, and promising to visit on his return. During the next few weeks, Carla became stronger. She was overjoyed that her idol had written to her, and this made her pain more bearable. Meanwhile every time Margaret met a pop star or an actor, she would get them to sign a get well card for Carla, and within a few weeks, Carla's bed was surrounded by bright cards from famous people.

It was about three months before Howard returned to England, but true to his word, he contacted Carla, and invited her to the Brighton Centre to see him in concert. It was a lovely day, and Carla had been so looking forward to it. They were taken onto the stage as the band was tuning up, and from nowhere, suddenly, there Howard was in front of her. 'Hallo Carla, how are you doing? I've been looking forward to seeing you.' At this Carla did not know whether to laugh or cry, and so did both. Howard sat with Carla for a couple of hours, talking about his tour and showing her photos of where he had been, besides showering her with gifts from various exotic places. She was in seventh heaven. 'It was the happiest day of my life,' Carla remembers. 'I thought I was going to be in hospital for ever, and I never thought Howard Jones would even remember me. It was wonderful.'

Carla made a good recovery from her injuries. She has the use of her limbs, and walks and runs like any other teenager, something her doctors and her family thought would never be possible after such a serious accident.

Helen Burton was 13 when doctors diagnosed cancer, and gave her three months to live. It was November 1982 when the bright teenager from Birmingham started to limp. Soon she could hardly lift her right arm, and her worried parents, Mick and Pauline, took her to hospital where x-rays and a biopsy at the Goodhope Hospital revealed that she had cancer in the muscles and tissue in her right ankle, right hip, right shoulder, and the left side of her head.

By February 1983, Helen had been transferred to Birmingham Children's Hospital, for intensive chemotherapy and radiotherapy. The doctors held out little hope, as the cancer was so widespread. The treatment took its toll. Helen reduced in size from a healthy eight stone to just four stone, half her body weight. She was so thin that although twelve months of treatment was prescribed nobody thought she would complete it.

Helen hated being in hospital. She suffered from all the side effects of the treatment. Her skin was sore, her mouth was full of ulcers, and she was deeply depressed. Margaret was making one of her routine telephone calls to the children's wards, when the Sister suggested that

Helen could do with some cheering up. It took only one telephone call to Helen, and her parents, for Margaret to leap into action.

Margaret was working on a treat that Helen would not forget. Telephone calls and letters flew round the country, and Margaret was undaunted by hitches. 'There's nothing I like more than a challenge. Someone just has to tell me I can't do something, and I'm off, doing it.' A few weeks went by, during which time Helen became a little stronger, and her ulcers cleared up enough for the doctors to decide she was well enough to travel. The Burtons left Birmingham, heading for the BBC Television studios in West London, where they were ushered into the control room in time to see Saturday morning's children's programme go out live. On screen was Helen's hero Boy George, and she was thrilled to think that he was so close by. After the programme, the producer took Helen and her parents and sister to the hospitality room and there he was in the flesh.

Boy George and Helen chatted for half an hour about music, and Helen was struck by his good humour. He asked her about her treatment, and went out of his way to make sure she had signed copies of his records to take away as a souvenir. Then the family was whisked off to the BBC canteen for some lunch with two of the Radio One disc jockeys, Mike Reid and Keith Chegwin. Helen's special day was a whirl of activity, and it stood her in good stead, for on her return to Birmingham, she once again had to go into hospital for more treatment.

'Meeting Boy George and my day in London cheered me up no end,' she says. 'It really helped me to get through more chemotherapy as I had such great memories.'

But there was yet another surprise up Margaret's sleeve for Helen. After she was discharged from hospital, her parents told her that she was going to London to have lunch with Margaret as a thank you for all her kindness. They arrived at the Holiday Inn, to be greeted by another familiar face, the jockey Bob Champion, who encouraged Helen to go on fighting and presented her with a toy dog from Dreams Come True, which Helen called Champ.

These days, Helen is a Youth Training Scheme trainee, at a home in Litchfield for children with special needs. Nobody could understand better than Helen the pain of being different, and for these children, many of whom have been battered, neglected, or who are just not as bright as most, she is a source of encouragement and strength.

Helen herself is in good emotional form, but her cancer has returned, this time in her right arm. But ever courageous, she has great hopes that as before, she will conquer it again. Illness has never stopped her in the past from succeeding; she has raised over £23,000 for the Birmingham Children's Hospital's Scanner Appeal by running discos and barbecues. Helen still has Champ, who is a constant reminder of how hard she battled to overcome her previous cancer.

People like Helen never fail to move Margaret, who remains continually impressed by the determination, courage and stamina of the children she comes into contact with. 'People often ask me if I feel excited to meet all these pop stars and actors, but I always reply that it's the children who really deserve my admiration. They are so special, they have incredible courage, and it's certainly an honour to meet them.'

There are also children whose incredible strength in face of terrible pain makes them miracles of courage. All the young people that Margaret makes happy have been through far more than any healthy person could ever imagine. The treatment for all these life-threatening diseases is radical. The side effects are usually more painful and unpleasant than the symptoms of the disease itself, and for many of the children, the agony goes on and on. That they survive, cheerfully, and that their families can carry on, faced with the effects of the treatment, is also a wonder.

One such child is Lesley Taylor, a charming and lively 15-year-old from Bideford. The younger of two daughters, Lesley now lives with her parents in the quiet Devonshire town, but in the last five years, she has only spent a matter of weeks at home while undergoing treatment and radical surgery for cancer.

Lesley was ten when she started to complain of a sore leg. Her mother, Marjorie, could see no sign of anything wrong, and thought that her daughter, like other children her age, was simply trying to avoid school. But Lesley continued to speak of the pain, and after a couple of weeks, she had started to limp. Marjorie Taylor decided to take her to the local doctor, but after a brief examination, his prognosis was that Lesley was suffering from growing pains. Marjorie, and her husband Brian, while being sympathetic and believing that she certainly must have a little discomfort to be complaining so much, tried to put it out of their minds. An aspirin occasionally would do the trick, they hoped.

But a week later, Lesley had a bad asthma attack, and while she was finding it hard to breathe, she was also crying from the pain in her leg. The doctor was called to the house, and this time a locum, a lady doctor in town for a few weeks only, examined the child. Her diagnosis was different, and she arranged for Lesley to have an x-ray straight away. 'We still thought it was growing pains,' confesses Marjorie. 'But this doctor seemed so competent that we took Lesley into the local hospital the next day.'

Lesley was put on a ward with other children, and as it was the end of the week, she was virtually alone as those who had had tonsillectomies and other ordinary childhood operations had been sent home. The consultant from Exeter was making his weekly ward round when he saw Lesley for the first time. The nursing staff explained she was suffering from growing pains, but after looking at the x-rays, he was very concerned. 'This child is not suffering from anything like growing pains. You're looking at something quite different on these x-rays. You're looking at a tumour on the thigh bone,' Dr Amin told them. 'I want to meet the parents. I think this child should see the experts in Bristol.'

Marjorie and Brian Taylor were stunned when Dr Amin explained what he had found. They could not really believe that their bright, lithe daughter could possibly be ill. 'It just doesn't hit you straight away. We didn't know any other children with this kind of thing. We'd never come across a child with cancer. We simply thought that Lesley must have knocked herself while playing netball. We just could not believe it.'

Within 24 hours, an ambulance had arrived, and mother and daughter were on their way to Bristol, to see the specialist. Marjorie remembers wandering around the house, unable to get her thoughts straight, and able only to pack some nighties for Lesley and a couple of dresses for herself. She had no idea at that point that this would be the beginning of a nightmare that would last five years.

They arrived late evening, and Lesley and Marjorie were taken straight up to the children's oncology ward. Nobody had told them what to expect, and the sight of children who were already undergoing treatment for cancer was shocking. The chemotherapy makes most people terribly sick, and they lose their hair. Some get very sore mouth and skin ulcers; patients look very ill indeed. For Marjorie, the sight of these very poorly children was a fright she had not expected. She looked at her pretty daughter, and could hardly bear the thought that if the biopsy Lesley would undergo the next day revealed that she did have cancer, she too would look like these poor children.

The results were all they feared. Lesley's tumour was malignant, and the treatment would have to begin at once. The other parents on the ward were wonderful to Marjorie, explaining to her what was to come, and gently helping her to come to terms with the reality of her child's illness. Lesley had a year's chemotherapy, and by the time her mother took her home, twelve months of treatment had caused a great change. The plump child was gone, and Lesley now weighed only three stone. Marjorie would carry her up and down stairs like a baby, and had to sponge her gently to avoid hurting her when she was being bathed. But even when she was very, very sick, Lesley remained cheerful. When anyone asked how she was, she would always reply, 'I'm fine, thank you, how are you?' She always had a smile for everyone, and never moaned.

In November 1983, Dr Martin Mott, the specialist at Bristol Hospital, recommended that Lesley travel to Birmingham Hospital for a revolutionary operation, which would replace her diseased bone with a metal plate. Unfortunately this was not a success, and her body rejected it. The tissue became infected, and the leg would swell and then burst. Lesley underwent operation after operation to clean out the wound, and was in constant pain. Because she was still growing, she also had to have operations to lengthen the bones of her leg, and this too caused searing pain.

'She was a brick,' says Marjorie. 'She never once complained of the pain, but I could see it in her face, and she would just nod when I'd offer her pain killers. I was so proud of her, and felt so helpless.'

For three and a half years, Lesley moved from Birmingham Children's Hospital to Woodland Hospital in Birmingham, returning occasionally to Bristol, with the odd weekend at home. It was a sad time for the Taylors. Brian, a stone mason, was alone at home, his older daughter had already moved into a flat of her own. Marjorie stayed with Lesley, and kept a lonely vigil round the clock.

Mother and daughter learnt to live with the pain. But when it got worse again Marjorie was sure that the cancer was back. Lesley, now nearly 14, would cry all night, and Marjorie would stay with her, holding her until the doctors gave her a pain-killing injection, and she would eventually sleep. By day, however, Lesley was her usual self, laughing with the nurses and the other children, and making everyone around her smile.

Marjorie begged the doctors at Woodland for another biopsy, but they said the pain was due to the lengthening operations. Eventually, when Lesley started to scream with the pain, they sent her back to Birmingham Children's Hospital, and after a biopsy, they found that the cancer had indeed returned, this time in the back of the leg. It was too late, they had no choice now but to amputate, and hope that they had taken all the cancer away. Even now, Lesley remained cheerful. 'I'm all right,' she told everyone. 'There are people far worse off than me.'

Lesley was sent back to Bristol, and was able to spend some time at home too, when she saw some of the girls she had been at school with, and their laughter would fill the house.

It was at this time that Marjorie heard about Dreams Come True. Both Birmingham and Bristol Children's Hospitals had come to know and like Margaret, and they had recommended to Marjorie that she drop a line to Dreams Come True; if anyone needed a treat to cheer them up, it was surely Lesley. It took only a few days for Margaret to telephone, and Marjorie felt immediately as if she had known her all her life. 'Margaret's an incredibly kind person with the biggest, most generous heart, and she has been such a comfort to me.'

Margaret wanted to know who Lesley would like to meet. Pop star Prince was the choice, but after numerous phone calls, it proved too difficult to arrange. But there was something else Lesley and Marjorie might enjoy. Montreux was coming up in May, perhaps they'd like to come? Lesley vowed she'd be well enough to travel, and five months after the loss of her leg, she was in Switzerland, having the time of her life.

She met pop star Paul Young, who told her that she had to keep on fighting. Lesley laughed and smiled more than ever, Marjorie recalls, and nobody could imagine that this happy girl had been through so much. Samantha Fox, in Montreux with her latest hit, could not believe that Lesley's leg had been amputated in January. At the disco on the last night, Lesley got onto the dance floor, and with a little help from her crutches, danced away the night.

'It broke my heart,' says Marjorie. 'Kids her age were going out, dancing every week, running around and having fun. All Lesley had known was pain, and hospitals. But there she was, having the time of her life. I nearly cried with the sheer joy and the pain of it.'

Afterwards Lesley could not stop talking about Montreux. The photos and T-shirts were all over her room at home, and she listened to the cassettes on her personal stereo. Her school friends enjoyed the tales of pop stars and Alpine evenings. But although Lesley seemed brighter than ever, Marjorie was worried; once again, she felt her child was ill. Marjorie telephoned Dr Mott, and begged him to scan her, just to be sure that all was well. Dr Mott was concerned about the radiation levels, but on Marjorie's insistence, because several months had elapsed since the amputation, Lesley went up to Bristol for a scan.

Lesley never returned. The scan revealed that the cancer had spread to her lungs, and she had yet again to undergo surgery. It was February 1988. She was very ill, and very weak but was able to laugh on her birthday in May. A scan in August revealed more cancer, this time in her right lung, and even then, with the prospect of still more surgery, Lesley Taylor kept in good spirits.

Now Marjorie often sees a wistful look in her daughter's eyes, for at 15, she is old enough to understand what is happening to her. The future for Lesley will no doubt include more pain. But everyone who has met her has been touched by her charm and her sheer joy in life, and her miraculous courage.

Debbie Powell from Clwyd in North Wales was a real Daddy's girl. She loved to go to the horse races with her father Ron Powell and, like him, she loved to ride; the sensation of speed was exciting for her. She went fishing with him too, and it was on one of these trips in 1983, that she first became ill. She was 14 at the time, and had started to cough badly. Much to her disappointment, Ron put an end to her getting cold and wet. He did not like the sound of her cough at all.

Only a few days later, Debbie found a lump on her neck, and her glands were swollen. When her mother took her to the GP, the diagnosis of glandular fever was made. But both Ron and Valerie were unhappy with Debbie's condition, and when she started to have difficulty breathing, they rushed her straight to Wrexham Hospital. It was a Sunday, and on the Monday, the doctors decided that the child should be transferred to Alder Hey Hospital in Liverpool. Within only a few hours, the specialists there told the Powells the worst news they had ever received. Debbie had cancer of the lymph glands, Hodgkin's Disease.

She was installed on the children's ward, and the treatment began. The chemotherapy made her, like everyone else, terribly sick. For six months, she had the drugs pumped into her system for three days a week, and then would be allowed home to recover. Her hair began to fall out in handfuls, and within only three months, she had lost most of it.

But Debbie seemed to pull back from the edge, and for a few months, she was well again. She was not able to ride her pony, but she could at least walk with her, and play with her dog and cat. She loved animals, and was never happier than when she was stroking her pony. But her good health did not last, and a few weeks later, Ron noticed that Debbie was not looking well again. Weight was dropping off her, and she was tired all the time. She had seemed so much better after the first treatment that the Powells could not believe that Debbie was declining again.

They telephoned Dr Martin at Alder Hey Hospital, told him they were worried, and in a matter of hours, she was back on the ward. For three months, it was touch and go. She dropped below four stone in weight, and Ron and Valerie thought that they might lose their youngest daughter. Valerie did not leave Debbie's side, keeping a constant vigil night and day. A sore on Debbie's back caused some concern, and this was removed. When another appeared almost at once, the doctors' fears were confirmed. The cancer was back, and Debbie would have to undergo more chemotherapy.

But there were bright spots too. Debbie's older brother Mark was to be married on 4 August 1984, and Debbie was the chief bridesmaid. The family begged her to be well enough to attend the wedding, and on the Saturday morning, she announced she felt well enough to go.

Dressed in her bridesmaid outfit, the hospital put her in a taxi with a nurse, and the congregation sobbed with delight as the brave 15-year-old walked down the aisle.

In November 1985, Debbie's treatment was over, and thin and tired, she was now home for good. She loved show jumping and was sad her father had sold her pony when she was so ill. Determined to ride again, Debbie fell off while jumping and broke her leg in two places. Her parents did not try to stop her from riding, but insisted that if she had to have thrills, then she had to race on the flat.

As a treat, Ron wrote to Henry Cecil, a well-known Newmarket trainer, and asked if he could bring Debbie down for the day. She loved it, and the day clinched her future. 'This is what I want to be, Dad. A jockey.' While the chemotherapy had made her very sick, one of its side effects is that growth becomes much slower and, in girls, hormone treatment is used to ensure they develop fully. Debbie was very light and petite; in her view, the perfect size for a jockey.

Back in Clwyd, Valerie had read about Margaret Hayles and wrote to her, asking if she could arrange for Debbie to meet her hero, show jumper Harvey Smith. Margaret was on the phone within days, wanting to know all about Debbie. And did she have a horse? Sadly, the pony had been sold on while Debbie was ill, and the courageous teenager was still riding other people's animals. 'Well, we'll have a whip-round for one, then,' announced Margaret.

Margaret was at Hickstead All England Show Jumping Arena chatting to a friend when it was suggested that she should contact businessman John Burbridge, the Managing Director of SR Direct Mail. When John heard about Debbie he agreed to give Margaret £1,000 for a horse for her. A few weeks later, Debbie's dream came true. She met Harvey Smith at Hickstead, and to her utter surprise and delight, he presented her with her very own horse, Holly, a 15-hand chestnut mare. This meant that now Debbie could start to train, and perhaps one day she would be good enough to join a racing stable. For two years, she rode Holly every day, enjoying the powerful horse, and getting stronger and fitter with each outing.

In November 1987, Debbie's ultimate dream came true. Trainer Bill O'Gorman, from Newmarket, took her on as a £35 a week apprentice jockey, and she loved it. It was not long before she started to date an apprentice at another stable. These days, Debbie Powell trains with Colin Williams's stable, also in Newmarket. She is fitter and happier than she has ever been. Her parents still find it hard to believe that the robust jockey they see on the gallops was once so ill that she was too thin even to lie down without pain.

That Kirsty Margotts survived the accident is a miracle in itself. The 12-year-old was on her way home from school, waiting on the platform for her train, when everything went black. Nobody knows what really happened, but Kirsty was probably struck by a train door and knocked unconscious. It was 25 September 1985; Vince Margotts was at work, and Chris Margotts had just collected her nine-year-old son Alistair from school.

Chris was not too worried when Kirsty was late. The kids often took a later train when there were lots of them. She had been home only a few minutes, though, when the police arrived to tell her there had been an accident. Within a short time, she had been taken to the Accident and Emergency Unit at Cuckfield Hospital, where Vince was already waiting. They remembered to tell the staff that Kirsty was allergic to penicillin. Then they were allowed to see their daughter.

'She looked like The Elephant Man,' remembers Chris.' 'Her head was so swollen, and one eye was already puffing up. I remember thinking that she looked as though she was wearing blue eyeshadow, and wondering why she had worn it to school. But it was the bruising coming through. It was just horrific.' Kirsty was in a deep coma, and on a respirator. The doctors told the Margotts that they were doing everything they could for the child, and soon they transferred her to the Intensive Treatment Unit.

For several weeks, Chris, Vince and Alistair kept watch over Kirsty. They had no idea what would happen, or if she would live. But they never gave up hope. Within a few weeks, Kirsty came off the ventilator, and her eyes started to open slightly. She made spastic movements and subconsciously tried to pull out her drip and other tubes. But that went away too, and although she was still in a light coma, doctors were able to transfer her to the children's ward at Cuckfield Hospital.

She had started to recognise people by touch. Her grandfather was a great favourite, as his bald head would make her heart beat faster. She also recognised certain sounds. Chris always wore court shoes, and as she walked to Kirsty's bed, the sound of the heels on the floor would make her heartbeat quicken.

It took many many weeks for Kirsty to recover. It was a long slow process, and she would be conscious for only a matter of seconds at first. She could not speak or swallow, and she was like a new-born baby. She did not recognise anyone as such, but later she remembered that she just knew she could trust her parents.

Margaret read about Kirsty in the local paper, and decided to pay a visit to the hospital. By now it was October, and Margaret suggested that a tape of various well-known people telling her to wake up might have some effect. For a few weeks, she carried a tape recorder wherever she went, and stars like Noel Edmonds, Cliff Richard, Wham, Cannon and Ball, Les Dawson, Paul Young and Rolf Harris, and some 20 more, recorded messages of hope. 'Come on Kirsty, get out of bed', 'You can do it, Kirsty', 'Wake up, Kirsty, it's a beautiful day'. Over and over and over, Chris played the tape to her daughter.

It did the trick, and Kirsty began to respond to the tape. Every time she regained consciousness, it was for a little longer, and each time, she heard nearly 30 celebrities wishing her well. Eventually she completely regained consciousness, and it was time for her to relearn everything that had been wiped out by the accident. Margaret decided that Kirsty needed a real treat to cheer her up, something she could work towards, and so once again, she got on the telephone.

Paul Young was playing at the Brighton Centre, not far from East Sussex. Kirsty's 12th birthday was on 6 December, and that week the whole family took off for Brighton. Kirsty had made incredible progress since the accident only three months before. She was walking, and had regained quite a lot of her speech. It was a day the family remembers fondly. 'It's a day we thought we'd never have,' remembers Chris. 'It did so much for all of us as a family. Having been through hell, it really brought us closer together than ever before.'

The Margotts arrived at the Brighton Centre, to see Paul preparing for the evening's performance. He went to no end of trouble to show them how everything worked, and took both Kirsty and Alistair under his wing. He was fascinated by how well Kirsty had done, and could hardly believe that the child who had been at death's door only three months earlier could be with him on that day.

After their tour, with the children clutching their gifts of cassettes and photos, the family made their way to the Royal Albion for tea with Margaret. Paul had finished all his business at the concert hall, and joined them too. It was certainly a day to remember, as they laughed and chatted happily for another couple of hours, before returning home.

Eleven months after the accident, Kirsty was struck down again, this time with meningitis. She was desperately ill, and so open to infection, that once more the Margotts thought their daughter might not survive. But the tape came into its own again as it helped her recover from that too. Kirsty was determined that if a train could not kill her, neither would an infection.

These days, Kirsty is 15, and is growing into a highly attractive young woman. She is determined to run cross country again for her school, but while she regains her strength, she has taken up the recorder. It was a very proud moment for her parents when she stood up in front of an audience at her school for delicate children, and played a piece faultlessly, in spite of the tremor she still has on her left side.

When a severe tummy ache laid Sarah Myatt low her mother Sue, a former nurse, did not worry too much about it at first, as half Sarah's class at school had had a tummy bug. Even when ten-year-old Sarah was sick, she was not too worried. It was summertime, June 1985, and there were a lot of viruses around. But when the symptoms persisted, Sue Myatt called in the GP, and he suspected pneumonia. Sarah was not really ill as such, but as a precaution, they took her along to the nearest casualty department at the John Radcliffe Hospital in Oxford.

It was while the family waited in the casualty department that Sue Myatt's fears grew. A very high temperature and severe abdominal pain suggested that Sarah had appendicitis. Suddenly, while waiting, Sarah went into shock. She was white as a sheet, sweating heavily, and was in great pain. Her abdomen became rigid. These were all the signs of something bursting in her abdomen. The staff were wonderful, and within minutes, Sarah, whom they thought had peritonitis or a burst appendix, was on the operating table.

When she was gone for several hours the Myatts knew that something serious was wrong. The registrar appeared finally, and took the Myatts aside. He had found a tumour the size of a melon on Sarah's ovaries, with secondaries in her stomach. She had lost a lot of blood, and she was very ill.

He had been unable to identify the type of tumour it was, and although he called in an oncologist from the other side of Oxford, they were still none the wiser. He suggested that they wait a few days, to see if the tumour revealed its type, and to allow Sarah to recover from surgery. The Myatts were in shock. Their daughter had not looked ill at all, and to be told she had cancer was horrific. They were taken to her bedside, and the reality of the situation was evident. She was pale as a white dove, with intravenous drips in both her arms; she looked as if she were at death's door.

The following few days were a blur of doctors and nurses, drips and tears. Finally, it was decided that Sarah was well enough to be moved, and the opinion was that she needed to be under the care of a consultant who specialised in this particular type of cancer. They suggested sending her straight to Great Ormond Street Hospital in London to the care of the consultant cancer expert, Dr John Pritchard. A very busy man, he agreed to look at the child, but he was honest. 'If I feel I can do anything for her, I will take on the case. If not, I'm afraid I will have to leave her to my highly respected colleagues in Oxford.' After his examination, he felt there was a 30 per cent chance that Sarah would live, and with that, treatment was underway. Within an hour, the child had been installed in a cot on the children's ward (they had no more beds) and Dr Pritchard had prescribed the chemotherapy she would have.

Sue Myatt was desperate. As a nurse, she had seen lots of people undergo chemotherapy, and she felt that if her child was so ill, it would be kinder to maintain her at home on pain relief, and not put her through the horrors of chemotherapy. She did not want to see her daughter suffer unnecessarily if she was going to die. But somehow, Dr Pritchard gave Sue great confidence and renewed strength, and they decided to go ahead.

The treatment was every bit as terrible as Sue had anticipated. Sarah was terribly weakened by the constant nausea and could not eat. Her weight dropped to two stone, and she was in constant discomfort. All her veins had been used up with the chemotherapy, and so they inserted a Hickman's catheter in her chest through which they could administer the drugs directly into the system. The catheter would go straight into a vein behind the breast bone. She had a gastric tube too, to feed food directly into her stomach to minimise the vomiting. Over those months, Sarah was so nauseated and debilitated by the treatment that it was not feasible for her to be home too much. She would collapse within hours of being home, and Sue and Bryan Myatt then had to take her straight back to Great Ormond Street. She would be terribly sick, and totally dehydrated, and sometimes new doctors did not recognise the symptoms, in spite of Sue's warnings; Sarah would literally pass out before the doctors would listen to Sue. On several occasions, Sue would just know that something was very wrong, and would rush to her daughter's bedside to see her choking or distressed. On two occasions, she had to resuscitate her.

Sarah was a great favourite with the nursing staff because she was such a contented child, and it was through a nurse at the John Radcliffe Hospital that Margaret met her. Margaret was organising a trip to Bournemouth on the Orient Express for several children and their families, and Sarah was invited too.

It was the first time she had been out for some fun since she had become ill, and although she was terribly skinny and very weak, it was a memorable day. They had brunch on the train, and magician and comedienne Jessica Martin kept everyone well amused during the journey. When the train got to Bournemouth, everyone piled out, and frolicked on the beach. Sarah and her brother Nick, a year older, and Sue took off their shoes and socks, and splashed around in the icy water. 'It was a real boost for everyone,' remembers Sue. 'It was just what we needed after the trauma of Sarah's illness.'

The day out was being filmed for TV-AM, and Sarah was one of the children to be selected for interview. Just as the presenter was ending the interview, she asked Sarah if there were any other dreams she might have. Quick as a flash, she told the country that she wanted to fly in a hot air balloon with Richard Branson.

A well-known balloon enthusiast, Richard was delighted to take Sarah up in his balloon. It was all set and the whole family turned out to watch the ballooning. Richard Branson had organised a cake for Sarah, made in the shape of a hot air balloon, with a little girl waving in the basket. Unfortunately, it was too blustery that day to fly, but everyone had a good tea, and there was plenty of laughter. Richard, a great supporter of Dreams Come True, telephoned Sarah several times to see how she was. In August 1988, Sarah and her family finally flew in a hot air balloon from Branson's house in Oxfordshire. 'He's really easy to talk to, and really funny and kind,' says Sarah. ' He let me help him with all the preparations, and it was just so exciting to fly over the fields.'

Today, Sarah Myatt is a healthy 13-year-old. She remembers the bad times of her illness, but is philosophical about the pain and the discomfort. 'I met Margaret through all of that, and I would never have been on the Orient Express or in Richard Branson's balloon if it hadn't been for her.' Sarah's cancer has gone, and as she lost only one ovary in surgery, she can look forward to a normal life.

Trudie Davies comes from the Rhondda Valley in Mid Glamorganshire, and to hear her lilting Welsh voice, you would never imagine that she has suffered from cystic fibrosis all her life. She is a chirpy, happy young woman with a huge energy for life.

Trudie has managed to lead a very full life, attending school, and working afterwards in a number of jobs, from a clerk in the County Council, to a barmaid in a wine bar. She had spent relatively little time in hospital. The odd infection had laid her low but, until she reached 19, she had been quite well.

At 19 she contracted a pseudomonas infection, a particularly insidious germ which becomes more serious with passing time. It's the bug that does most of the harmful damage to cystic fibrosis sufferers, as there are no antibiotics which specifically deal with it. So while Trudie Greaves, as she was then, was not feeling too bad, the bug was working on her system. But by the time she reached 23, the disease was beginning to take hold. Her spells in hospital were more frequent, and each infection was more serious than the one before. Trudie's veins were becoming used up; they were very thin and hard, and it was becoming almost impossible to put lines into her. There were stomach problems too, caused by the pancreas dysfunction, and because her food was poorly digested, there were frequent blockages.

But although she was feeling less well, she was still working, and it was while she worked in a wine bar that she met Keith Davies. It was 26 January 1985, and they met across a crowded, smoke-filled bar. Exactly one year later to the day, Trudie and Keith became engaged.

Trudie was very active in her local Brownies, and was a Tawny Owl. Her best friend, Barbara Williams, was a Brown Owl, and the two girls virtually ran their local group. Barbara knew of Trudie's fondness for Cliff Richard, and she had written to Dreams Come True on her friend's behalf, asking if it would be possible for Trudie to meet him.

For Trudie's birthday, Barbara organised a mock *This Is your Life*, and as each guest was announced, the Brownies would clap and giggle. Finally, she told Trudie that there was a message from someone she did not as yet know, but whom she had always wanted to meet. It was a card from Margaret, saying that a meeting would soon be arranged. Trudie was overcome.

Trudie Greaves and Keith Davies were to be married on 26 July 1986, in St Barnabas Church at Penygraig. Various meetings had had to be cancelled due to poor health, but the week before the wedding, Margaret telephoned Barbara and asked if Trudie was free on the Saturday. 'No, she's getting married that day,' she replied.

The wedding was a beautiful affair, with 70 guests in church, and 100 at the do in the evening. The best man, Geoff Williams read out the messages, and he came to almost the last one. 'I have a special card here from someone I know you'd like to meet,' he said. It was from Cliff Richard. There was a gasp around the room, and Trudie was delighted. The next card was from Margaret, offering Trudie and Keith two weeks' honeymoon in September – the first time Keith had been able to take leave – in a luxury caravan near Interlaken. Trudie was, for the first time in her life, speechless. That was a dream she had never imagined could come true.

Everything about the holiday was wonderful. Margaret met them at Gatwick Airport with the tickets before they left, and Trudie remembers that it was just like meeting an old friend. They were a short stroll from Lake Thon, and each day they would feed the ducks, have a swim in the icy water, and sightsee. It was idyllic.

Cliff had not forgotten her, and soon after their return from Switzerland, Margaret arranged for them to travel to London to see him in *Time* at the Dominion Theatre, London. They arrived a little early for the matinee, and Margaret met them at the station, and took them for lunch. Then it was the moment to meet Cliff. 'He was wonderful,' remembers Trudie, 'really normal, very chatty, and so kind.' The show was good too, and the day was etched in their minds for ever.

Trudie Davies spends more and more time in hospital these days, but whenever she feels depressed, she thinks of those times. Her lovely husband Keith is a great support. But the memory of that honeymoon, and her meeting with Cliff Richard, boosted her morale sky-high.

*

Four-year-old David Gladwin had not been well for some time, and repeated visits to the doctor had proved fruitless for his mother Carol. David had had trouble with his digestive system, and had fairly constant diarrhoea since he was two. Carol felt that David was really not well, and insisted that he had something more seriously wrong with him.

She took him to Basildon Hospital in Essex, and the doctors decided that as his tummy was so swollen and tender they should take some x-rays, and a blood test. His stomach was full of fluids he should have excreted, and the blood test showed up some abnormalities. After some immediate surgery to drain his stomach, David was transferred to St Bartholomew's Hospital in London.

A scan showed that there was something growing on his kidney. An immediate biopsy revealed that the tumour was malignant, and so David was started on chemotherapy and radiotherapy that would continue for some eighteen months. David became desperately thin, very sick, and of course his hair fell out.

For his mother, it was a very difficult time. She had two older children, and an eight-month baby to look after, and with her husband John at work, it was a matter of enlisting her mother and her sister to help out. Everyone was very tired, and very drained by David's illness, but the bright little boy carried on, and lifted everyone's spirits. When people in the street would stare, David would always have an appropriate quip. In hospital, he was a friendly, helpful child. If a new child was on the ward, he would show him or her his scar — his zipper, he called it — and say it did not really hurt and everything would be just fine.

In January 1986, Carol Gladwin met Margaret through another mum, Jan Roberts, whose little girl, Helen, had leukaemia. Helen had wanted to wash the elephants at Whipsnade Zoo; she arrived for her big day togged out in waterproofs and wellies, and complete with a nailbrush which the keepers encouraged her to use to scrub the elephant's soft grey trunk. Helen had made good progress, and Jan suggested that Margaret might like to give David a treat. It took a quick telephone call for Margaret to discover that what he would really like to do was to fly like Peter Pan.

Fortunately, singer Bonnie Langford was in pantomime in Brighton, as Peter Pan. Perfect, thought Margaret. The whole Gladwin family turned up at the theatre in Brighton in late January, and David was very excited. Bonnie had found him a Peter Pan hat, and within moments, the two of them were flying through the air. There were squeals of delight, tinged with a little fear, as they were whisked high into the rafters. After David's acrobatics, they all watched the panto. It was a lovely outing.

Back at Barts, the doctors decided to try to remove the rest of David's tumour surgically, but it was too embedded. He would have another course of chemotherapy instead. By November 1986, a scan revealed that the tumour had gone. Today David Gladwin is a healthy eight-year-old.

7

The Letters

Sale
Greater Manchester

Dear Billy [Joel],

I would like to thank you for helping me through the hardest days of my life, whilst I was on chemotherapy, for listening to you gave me such infinitesimal pleasure and helped me to carry on,

Yours truly,

Mark [Harris]

Headington
Oxford

Dear Margaret

I would like to thank you so much for taking me to
Blackpool and a very big thank you for the concert the
other night it was really smashing, and all the photos you
took of me and the stars for me to look at cheer me up
when I'm down.

So a big, big, big thank you, you're great and I love you
very much and so does my family for giving me such a
boost.

All my love,

Lou [Louise Balhatchet] xxx

PS. Say hi to Simon from me please as he's a brilliant
photographer xxx.

Headington
Oxford

Dear Maggie

How are you? As you know I'm back in hospital starting treatment again as I'd had a relapse. But I would like to thank you for helping me by taking me to meet pop stars, by starting a fund in my name, the 'Louise Balhatchet' fund, but putting it into your fund so you can give other sick children a morale booster by taking them on trips and meeting pop stars.

I would like it if I could help raise money for your fund. I could help raise money for your fund. That would help me if I knew that sick children could benefit like I had.

Well I must go, all my love,

Lou xxx

Barnstaple
North Devon

Dear Margaret

Just a few lines trusting you and all the family are keeping well. Now that Sean [Steel] has gone I feel I must write and thank you once again for the lovely holiday we had — something I would never have been able to do for Sean.

I have my pictures to look back on when I feel a bit low and to reflect on all the lovely people we met, and the lovely times we both had. I also feel much richer for getting to know you, Nicky and Sy.

Sometimes I know it all gets you down and you feel people take things for granted, when after all it is only the children's happiness that matters. But please keep up the good work. They deserve all the happiness they can get in their short lives, and without wonderful people like yourself who really care it would just not be possible.

If at any time you want to have a break and get away for a few days, when things seem a bit heavy, just pack your toothbrush and find your way down to Devon. The door is always open, and our home will always be your home. We would really like to see you any time.

I will draw to a close now. Give all my love to everyone. God bless and take care.

Love,

Jess xxxxxx

Allesley
Coventry

Dear Margaret,

I lost my little girl Paula in August. I am writing to say thank you for the holiday to Sweden and Santa World. My two children Anna and Mark loved it, and I did too. The whole trip was absolutely wonderful.

We had never been abroad before. I took Paula in my heart — we lit a candle for her in a church in Sweden. I met Eileen and Graham who had lost a baby called Eleanor not so long ago. You sent them too. We got on very well, and are going to keep in touch.

We had two sweatshirts delivered yesterday from Dreams Come True. Thank you for those too. I have been asked to write a piece about the holiday for the church magazine.

If I can ever help you in any way please let me know. You are welcome to call if ever you are in Coventry — I really mean that!

With love from Margaret, Anna and Mark Britton

Mount Merrion
County Dublin

Dear Margaret

Since I've returned from Montreux I've been meaning to write to you, firstly to thank you so much for all the behind-the-scenes work that made the trip possible and secondly, to impress on you the value of the trip to both the children and their parents.

Most of the children on the trip had been receiving really gruelling treatment in the recent past – indeed some of them are still on treatment for their cancer. These are children who were perfectly normal and healthy not so long ago, and for some reason – unbeknownst to us – have been struck down with life-threatening illness. These illnesses have robbed the children of some of their most precious years, and being old enough to understand the nature of their disease, they must also face the uncertainty their future holds, and understandably often become very depressed and isolated, and so often feel the futility of going through a treatment that has no guarantee of a cure.

They worry, as would you and I, about possible relapses etc. You can't fob them off, as you can with younger children saying, 'This is to make your bad cells go away etc.' They also know what savaging long-term effects their treatment can cause — stunted growth, infertility, to name but a few.

This all brings me to tell you how much a special holiday like Montreux means to these kids. It is so different from anything they've ever done. First, they're going away with people who fully understand their disease, and so many of the other kids have been through similar treatment — it really gives those who are on treatment hope, and indeed courage, to battle on. I think this was reflected by Sharon not wearing her wig most of the time — she knew that everyone would accept her, and was secure enough in our company to leave it off. In most cancer units in the UK there are not that many teenagers in at any one time, so it is hard for them to communicate with each other quite openly about their cancer, which for some of them was quite a novelty — again reflected by the way they talked about it on the coach on the second day.

The holiday was indeed a 'once in a lifetime' trip for them — it was something none of their friends had ever done, giving it more status! For all of them it was the first holiday they had had since they were first diagnosed, and they felt privileged instead of pitied.

It was also marvellous for some of their parents to come along — for them the treatment has been every bit as harrowing. They have felt every needle their child has endured, and so often they have had to be the one to persuade the child to keep on fighting. These parents are every bit as deserving as their courageous kids. It will often be the only time they'll ever spend with their child alone, out of a hospital enviroment. I know from the mums who went this year that it's been one of their most treasured times and for some of them, by next year memories are all they'll have as some of their kids won't make it.

For me, as a nurse on a cancer unit, it gave me encouragement – it can be hard often to give drugs you know will make the kids violently sick. However, it gave me hope – at least seeing the kids make the most of their time in between treatments makes treatment justifiable.

Margaret, for all your work making 'Dreams Come True' thank you so much.

Cliona
Great Ormond Street Hospital, Ward 3AB

Burgess Hill
West Sussex

Dear Margaret

Thank you so much for arranging for Simon Trevor-Wilson to meet Rod Stewart. He has always adored Rod and it was his life's ambition to meet him – since then he has been so very happy. Rod was wonderfully kind to him, even inviting him back the next day to meet his family, giving him presents and photos, and making sure he had a marvellous time.

You would have thought they had been friends for years! Rod even gave him his home address so that they could write to each other. I don't think Simon will get over the excitement and emotion of those two days – they were the happiest of his life, and he can't wait to see the photos you took of them together. I don't think Simon or I could ever thank you enough for what you have done for him, and I wish you every success in the future with your charity.

Good wishes. Yours,

Lise Bishop

Raffles Avenue
Carlisle

Dear Margaret

How are you ? My mam is very ill and now the doctor says she will not get much better, and I am staying with my aunties round the corner until we know what is what.

Sometimes I feel like running away, or that when I wake up it will all be gone away. A dream of mine which will never come true is to have my mam well again. There is not one day that goes by that I do not see my mam going through pain. Sorry my letter is a mess. If only I lived close to you. I think of you as an auntie I love. I wish I could see you again. Writing this has taken some of my pain away.

On a happy note, on 31st March I went to see A-Ha at the Edinburgh playhouse. It was wonderful. I was on the back row, so I didn't see much, but tears came to my eyes again. Margaret, I hope you do not mind me asking but when you go to Switzerland may I write a letter to Morten [Harket]? I think he is one of my friends – he has brought me though my illness by playing his LP over and over. If this can be done please write and let me know so I can do it.

This letter has taken me one and a half hours to do. Please write very soon. I miss you – may I call you Auntie Margaret? Give my love to Nikki and all. Thank you for reading this messy letter.

Lots of love, Julie [Crawford] xx.

Raffles Avenue
Carlisle

Dear Auntie Margaret

I hope you are well. I am OK just now. I still miss my mam. I feel so empty inside, I love her so very much. I'm sore inside because I cannot tell her how very much. I am very happy to have an aunty like you. I wish my dreams would come true so I could see you again.

I have sent you a Cross for your pocket. Will you think of me when you look at it? Also a bookmark called Foot Prints, also the photos of me as I am now and one with my heroes. I have a carboard cut-out of A-Ha now. Well I will go now.

Please write soon. I will look forward to hearing from you.

Lots of love, Julie [Crawford] xx.

PS. Say hello to Nikki from me.

The Royal Marsden Hospital
Sutton
Surrey

Dear Mrs Hayles

Robert Campbell and his mother told me about your charity and gave me some of the information and pamphlets concerning Dreams Come True and it seems such a marvellous idea.

It is quite clear that for children who are suffering the consequences of a terrible disease, particularly cancer, the opportunity to fulfil a dream of meeting somebody famous, or doing something that would otherwise be impossible, must be a really important diversion away from their problems and can only bring benefit to them and the attempts to control their disease.

I am also particularly impressed with the way you clearly involve the parents in these ventures because they, of course, have all the stresses of their sick child and the opportunity to see happiness under these circumstances must be very rewarding.

I will distribute your leaflets in our two relevant wards

and I will be delighted if at any time in the future you would like me to help you in any tangible way. I wish you well.

With very kind regards,

R L Powles
Chairman, Division of Medicine, Physician in Charge, Leukaemia Unit

Bristol Royal Hospital for Sick Children
Bristol

Dear Mrs Hayles

I am writing to express the appreciation of members of the unit for the wonderful work that the Dreams Come True charity has been undertaking with some of our children who have cancer. It does not seem to matter whether they have recovered from their illness and treatment, and are getting back to a normal life, or whether indeed their treatment has failed and they are actually dying from their disease. In either case they seem to get an enormous psychological boost from their trip and it is clearly a highlight of their young lives.

We have found that it makes a considerable difference to them and would like to encourage you by letting you know how worthwhile it is. We hope that, thanks to your efforts, the charity will go from strength to strength in this good work.

With best wishes. Yours sincerely,

Martin G Mott
Consultant Paediatric Oncologist

Royal Liverpool Children's Hospital
Alder Hey
Liverpool

Dear Mrs Hayles

I would like to write and thank the charity Dreams Come True for all the work they have done for our patients with cystic fibrosis. Cystic fibrosis is a severe inherited disease that causes recurrent respiratory infections and failure to thrive, and even with adequate treatment, many children do not survive into adult life and the chances of going away to different parts of the world have greatly helped in boosting the morale of these children and their families.

Many of our patients come from deprived areas of Liverpool and without charity support it would be impossible for them to have a holiday at all, let alone to such exotic places that you have sent the children to. Already this year children have gone to the Dutch bulb festival, to a concert in Switzerland, a trip on the QE2 and the Orient Express, a trip to Denmark and a trip to Norway. A few of the older girls have met their idols, Phil Collins and Paul Young. I believe further holidays were offered but because of ill health, some children were unable to take up these holidays.

Yours sincerely,

D P Heaf
Senior Lecturer in Child Health
Respiratory Medicine

Royal Liverpool Children's Hospital
Alder Hey
Liverpool

Dear Mrs Hayles

I am delighted to support your charity Dreams Come True. As we all know, it is most important to give children with malignant disease goals to aim at, and contact with well-known pop stars, and unusual trips that would otherwise not be available to them, certainly fulfil this aim. As we are all well aware, it is not only the children themselves who need support, but the parents and brothers and sisters.

I do hope that your charity will go from strength to strength.

Yours sincerely,

John Martin
Consultant Paediatrician

Stourport on Severn
Worcestershire

Dear Mrs Hayles

I am writing to thank you for your letter of condolence which arrived soon after our son Leon's death. I sincerely regret the delay in replying to you as I have found it difficult to write of our loss. However, I felt I must write to you and thank you for arranging the trip on Concorde for Leon. He looked forward to it so much in the preceding weeks and I'm convinced he only lived as long as he did with the expectation to cling to.

Leon enjoyed the flight so much, the attention he received and the thrill of the day. Sadly he died four days later but I know he was still filled with the excitement right up until his death, as he proudly showed the things he had from the flight to everyone, including the doctors and nurses at the hospital.

Thanks once again for making a brave boy so very happy, and for memories that his family will treasure forever.

Yours sincerely,

Janet and Steve Burford

The Society of Parents of Children with Cancer
Solihull
West Midlands

Dear Margaret

Sadly I have to tell you that Leon Burford died in his sleep last Wednesday night, but I do know that Concorde was the very best thing that had happened to him. As you know he was extremely poorly before he went on his very much wanted and very much needed trip. Leon was so thrilled with the day and how marvellous the Captain and his wonderful cabin crew were to him. Most of all, he treasured the trip's original passenger sheet amongst other prized possessions that they gave to him. I was told that it seemed as if Leon waited for his dream to come true before he died. I wonder if you would be kind enough to pass on the sad news to the Concorde staff. He was an exceptionally brave young man and will be so sadly missed by all who knew him.

Yours sincerely,

Julia Wood

Dunfermline Bay
Fife

Dear Margaret

I feel as if I'm always writing to thank you, as yet again I'm writing to thank you for the really fantastic time I had at the Wet, Wet, Wet concert last night – it was absolutely wonderful. Unfortunately, we didn't get to meet the band. Maybe one day!

I hope Lindsay has recovered from her work with Mark. Margaret, my friends and I have started to arrange a disco in aid of Dreams Come True. I was wondering if you could send us some posters please ? Must go and put up my Wet, Wet, Wet poster – I think above my head so that I can keep an eye on Marti (all the time).

See you soon, lots of love,

Maria Taylor

Allesley
Coventry

Dear Margaret

Sorry for the delay in writing, but we have been in and out of hospital since our big day with you. I would like to thank you for again making Ryland so happy – he still has it on his mind every day, and is always on about Nigel [Mansell].

I have sent some photos which I hope you will like. Today a video came from Central TV which is lovely, and is being played over and over. Ryland is going back into hospital on Thursday for more treatment, which we are not looking forward to. He went on the scanner last week, and Dr Mann was a bit disappointed. After two treatments, although it hasn't spread any more the tumour hasn't got any smaller, which she was hoping for.

Although I do try to carry on as normal it is very hard, and at times I feel I can't go on any more – although I know I have to. Ryland has written to Nigel. I do hope he has the time to answer.

I saw you on television last week, and saw the joy you gave them, which helped me relive the joy which you brought into our lives. I hope you don't mind if I keep writing and telling you what is happening. I will write again after Ryland is out of hospital.

Love,

Sandra Dowse

The Society of Parents of Children with Cancer
Solihull
West Midlands

Dear Margaret

I am very pleased to report that when I saw Ryland this lunchtime, he was much improved. Not quite out of the woods yet, but certainly much better than his poorly state over the weekend. I did telephone Nigel Mansell's press secretary as soon as I had finished talking to you this morning. Unfortunately she wasn't about and I left a message with another charming answering machine. By the time I reached the Children's Hospital later at about 9.20, the wonderful Nigel had already telephoned Ryland, in fact had got him out of the bath. Apparently, Ryland tells me, Nigel is off to Italy tomorrow so methinks we got him just in time. It certainly put a smile back on Ryland's face, not to mention the Sister on the ward!

Kind regards,

Julia Wood

London

Dear Margaret

I would like to thank you from the bottom of my heart for organising for me to meet Gary Wilmot. I understand that it couldn't have been very easy to organise the chance for me to meet Gary. I enjoyed the show very much and even got to meet Gary after the show and get his autograph. I enjoyed everything a great deal so I would like to wish you a big thank you. I appreciate your hard work in arranging the tickets. I thought of it as a very nice favour and gesture for you to organise the show, and I would like to say a big thank you.

Lots of love,

Shaminder Rai xxxxx

Uxbridge
Middlesex

Dear Margaret

Just a quick note to say I think what you are doing for ill children is great. I would love to be able to follow your example and become a 'Mrs Fix-it', and help ill/terminally ill children. You should be sainted and Paul Young too. Karen has really picked up the good life since we met Paul Young and this is thanks to you. You are great, giving Karen the experience of being by her favourite pop star.

Thank you for the meeting and for giving Karen something to fight for. I could praise you for ever, but you have got other things to do.

Thank you,

From Emma

Handcross
Sussex

Dear Margaret

You will never know how much you have changed my
life. One minute I'm having horrendous treatment for
cancer, and the next I'm kissing Mark King [Level 42] at
the Prince's Trust concert, or am at Montreux or dancing
with the stars at the Dreams Come True ball. Finally
thank you for letting me come to your house whenever I
like and including me as part of your family.

Lots of love,

Sandra [Bailey] xxx

8

Margaret's Dreams

So far, Margaret has made over a thousand children very happy. She has given them and their families a very precious memory, something to treasure when times are both good and bad. And yet there seems to be no end of children still dreaming of that special person, or that special trip, that would make their treatment easier to bear, and give them and their families, a goal to aim for. But what of the pressure she feels?

Margaret is on call all day long, every day, for children and parents alike, in sickness, health, and grief. She shares every minute of their sorrow, and joins with them in their joy. She copes because she has to cope, because there is always another child waiting for her, and to disappoint one is not part of her philosophy.

But making dreams come true has not been without its traumas, and Margaret has shed many tears in the last six years. Certainly, there have been tears of sadness, but also tears of happiness, with a feeling of total fulfilment in a job well done. She cried the day 15-year-old Julie Crawford from Newcastle, a cancer victim who recovered only to watch her mother die from cancer, met her idol Morten Harket of the pop group A-Ha at the Montreux Rock Festival. Julie told him she loved him, and afterwards, she was so grateful to Margaret that she just cried with joy; Margaret was so moved by the teenager's ecstasy that she was unable to speak.

Margaret cried for Kelly Bennett, a courageous nine-year-old with cystic fibrosis, from Nottinghamshire, whose greatest wish was to make a record with David Essex. After only a few minutes' rehearsal, she sang beautifully, and cut a disc any performer would be proud of. They even printed up a special cover, with her name on it. 'To see that little thing with her headphones on, singing like a bird – it was wonderful.' David Essex is still in touch with the family.

There was the evening that Simon Trevor-Wilson met Rod Stewart after his concert in Brighton. Rod was delighted to meet the youngster, who had been crippled with spasticity since birth, and made him the centre of attention at his private parties on two nights running.

There is nothing too big for Margaret to attempt. Failure is not part of her make-up, and she rarely takes no for an answer. Pauline Benn from Cumbria, a teenager with spina bifida, was a great fan of American pin-up David Hasslehoff, of the TV series *Knight Rider*. Pauline had every picture and every poster at home, and watched videos of the programmes all day. She adored the handsome actor. Margaret decided to give her the surprise of her life. Pauline and her family came down to London for what she thought would be a weekend of sightseeing. But the morning after they arrived, a car whisked them off to the airport, where they left for Los Angeles. They were taken to the Burbank studios, where *Knight Rider* was being filmed, and David Hasslehoff spent an afternoon with his great fan. Indeed, Pauline appears in a scene of one episode of the programme. That was something she will certainly never forget – and nor will Margaret.

There is no treat too small, either. Michelle Whitham from Sheffield had lost both her eyes from cancer, and wanted a fluffy pussy cat more than anything else in the world. Margaret found one, and took it by coach, nestled on her lap, all the way from Sussex to Yorkshire. The seven-year-old was thrilled with the kitten, who became Michelle's constant companion until she died six months later.

Matthew Spice from Tewkesbury in Gloucestershire wanted 'a fluffy cat like his grandfather's' too. It was in fact a Blue Persian he wanted, and Margaret had one flown free of charge from Essex to the little boy's home town.

Three-year-old Katie Hendrie from Lewes in East Sussex sobbed for hours when the family dog died while she was in hospital having chemotherapy for leukaemia. All she wanted was another puppy-dog, as she called it, so her aunt contacted Margaret, and asked if the charity would make a donation towards the new pet. Margaret went one better. While receiving a cheque for £6,000 from Marks and Spencer for Dreams Come True, she mentioned young Katie's dream. Immediately, M&S offered to buy the child a King Charles spaniel – now called Bella – and yet another wish was accomplished.

Timmy Armstrong, from Aylesbury in Buckinghamshire, a four-year-old also with leukaemia, wanted nothing more than to dress up as a guard at Buckingham Palace. Wearing a miniature Guards uniform and complete with his own tiny Guards box, Timmy stood alongside the Queen Mother's guards at Clarence House, and loved every minute of it.

Thirteen-year-old Sarah Fenney from Manchester, who was very ill with cystic fibrosis, wanted to dance with ballerina Briony Brind at Covent Garden. On the day, the child wore her own tutu, and sat on a chair as Briony danced especially for her.

Two teenage cystic fibrosis sufferers, Michael and Daniel Strohm, wanted to fly in a microlite with Roger Daltrey. The former Who star spent the day with the boys, took them on a tour by air of his home and his farm, and nothing was too much trouble.

For cancer victim 13-year-old Caroline Hart, who lived in Burgess Hill in Sussex, a ride on the Grand National winner Aldiniti really helped hasten her recovery. And when Nottingham lad Stephen Joseph, aged 12, played chess with Nigel Short, the UK number one, he completely forgot about his cystic fibrosis as he concentrated on the game in hand; Stephen lost the game after a fierce defence, but was then able to pick up tips during a lesson with Nigel, who went on to present him with a leather chess set.

Margaret believes that nobody can really imagine what children like Timmy and Katie, Pauline and Simon, Matthew and Michelle, Michael and Daniel, Caroline and Stephen, and all the others go through. Nothing can describe the agony of treatment, the emotional distress of knowing that they may not survive, and the despair of the parents who can do nothing but sit and watch. In a way, Margaret offers hope, relief, understanding and happiness to a few.

She trusts fervently that the children who die go somewhere better. 'I believe in heaven, and if I didn't, I'd be in the local asylum. After all, these kids have never done anything wrong to anyone, so God must be saving them for something better. And I believe in God. This is a beautiful world, filled with the most glorious mountains and oceans, animals and flowers. If only people would stop whining, and get on with life, it'd be a much happier place.'

People in general have been very good to Dreams Come True, and to Margaret herself. There have been ups and downs, and some people who have been involved with the charity haven't always agreed with her methods and philosophy — nor she with them. There have also been those who have tried to become involved with the charity for their own ends, but they too are gone.

Margaret lives in a rented house, and works from her front room; she hopes to move soon to a larger place where she will be able to have more children to visit. Simon Callagan, Margaret's constant companion, is always a great support. He drives her the length and breadth of the country to see children, and is there to rub her tired shoulders when the load becomes too heavy. Her children help when they can too, and are proud to have her as their mum. 'She's the best mum in the world,' they say.

Dreams Come True now has two fund-raisers: Wendy Burdett, who also acts as a courier on the trips, and Jackie McLauchlin. Between them, they scour the country for money to help send children on magical tours that give everyone so much pleasure. The children love the publicity, too, when their local papers write up their stories. For a child who is ill, indeed for every child, it is a thrill to be seen in a photo with your hero – especially when all your friends see it too.

Everyone seems ready to give up their time for the charity, from high-powered businessmen who try to find funds, to the famous people the children want to meet. No one has ever refused to meet a child, unless they find it too upsetting, and these people are very few and far between. Many celebrities keep in touch with families long after the dream has come true.

Gary Numan has made two boys incredibly happy. Eighteen-year-old Terry Martin, wheelchair-bound with spina bifida, met Gary at his recording studios. Gary taught the youngster three notes on the synthesiser, and told him when to play them. On the back of Gary Numan's *Warriors* album, Terry Martin has a credit as a member of the band. And as if that were not enough, he later gave Terry his own synthesiser. Gary took Barry Cousins, an 18-year-old with cystic fibrosis, from Newcastle, for a day's flying in his aircraft. Gary still telephones to see how he's getting on.

Nigel Mansell has often taken young Ryland Dowse, a 13-year-old who has been struck with cancer for the second time, for spins in his fast racing cars. He keeps in touch with Ryland from wherever he is, and if the child is having a bad time, will always try to cheer him up. For all the children, like Ryland, encouragement from someone they admire is a huge boost to their morale.

When told of the poorly condition of Amanda Kettle, who was dying from a brain tumour, singer Alvin Stardust, promptly put down the cup of tea he was drinking and drove for three hours to be at Amanda's bedside in Stratford-upon-Avon. Unable to speak to Alvin, the 21-year-old girl lay in raptures as he sang to her. As she slipped into unconsciousness for the very last time she beamed happily at Alvin, who responded: 'I love your smile.' Amanda died shortly afterwards, and her parents felt they could not thank Alvin enough for making their daughter's final moments so complete.

Margaret can only say: 'Most people I ask for help from are absolutely marvellous and are such sincere and warm people. Pop stars and sports personalities have given endlessly of their time, while many firms and businesses and quite ordinary people have helped give me the resources I need to make these dreams come true. I can't think of anyone who has not been impressed and humbled by the strength and bravery of these young people. The price these children are paying for life itself is such that any time and money we spend in helping them is insignificant in comparison.'

Margaret's own dreams are very simple, and some have already come true. She now enjoys personal happiness, and is surrounded by the people who truly care for her. Her love of animals is well rewarded. She lives with her fluffy Persian cat Sacha, who is soon to have a friend, as well as nine rabbits, and three Shetland ponies. Two of the ponies were given to her by a great supporter of Dreams Come True, Lady Fisher, who owns Kilverstone Wildlife Park, and who often receives children for a day out. Bubbly and Lullaby have been a tremendous success, and have been joined by Pickles, a very placid Shetland that Margaret bought for £100. Visiting children – and there are many of these – can ride Pickles round the fields at the back of the house.

Margaret runs an open house, and children and parents are welcome to come and visit, play with the rabbits, and enjoy the country. Several children have virtually become members of the family, and now Margaret can hardly remember a time without the frequent visits of Sandra

Bailey, Mark Simpson, Helen Meaden and Edward French. She holds wedding receptions for some of those she helps in her beautifully tended back garden. Margaret tries always to be available for solace and understanding, advice and help at any time.

Margaret herself loves her home, and gets up very early to enjoy the peace of the countryside, chat to her animals, and have time to think before the phone begins to ring. She believes that you only ever get out of life what you put in. On that score, she must be well ahead of the rest, as she contributes 100 per cent to the lives of so many.

And what of the future for Dreams Come True? There are people in Belgium, Germany, Canada and New Zealand who want to set up branches in their countries. In the very near future, it is hoped that children will meet Bruce Springsteen, Michael Jackson, Sylvester Stallone and Jean Michel Jarre. A child from Belfast will go to America to see Michael Crawford in *Phantom of the Opera*, and of course in the pipeline there are the now legendary trips to Montreux, Santa World, and Legoland. Latest news is that trips being planned for 1989 include skiing in Austria and a visit to the Channel Islands.

Meanwhile, Margaret remains the driving force behind Dreams Come True; an undaunted one-woman band with tireless energy and enthusiasm, plus a big heart and a will to enrich the lives of young people who have been through so much. Of course she tires, but one look at the joy on a child's face is enough to banish any doubt about what she is doing, and will continue to do.

The children Margaret helps are very special children, and have a wisdom and serenity beyond anything ordinary people know. They enrich the lives of everyone they touch, they have a humour and generosity of spirit far beyond their years, and courage and determination that would put most of us to shame. Their families believe they have been blessed to know and care for them, and Margaret believes she too is blessed to be able to give them laughter and joy on their special day.

Acknowledgments

Special thanks to all the parents and children who patiently told me their stories, shared their deepest feelings with me and who have kindly granted me the privilege of recounting their experiences.

Thanks to Margaret, for her time, encouragement and humour.

Thanks to my father, Dr Jack Davidson, for patiently explaining and checking all the medical explanations, and to my nearest and dearest for tolerating me while writing what has been a rewarding, enriching, but emotionally difficult book.

And last, but by no means least, thanks to Jenny Parrott, at Bloomsbury, for her help and words of wisdom.

ABOUT THE AUTHOR

Lisa Davidson is a journalist who has worked on current affairs and documentary television programmes in the U.K. and Australia for many years.

She first met Margaret Hayles in 1985 while working for the BBC; later Lisa made a documentary on Dreams Come True and Margaret for TVS. They have remained close friends. Lisa is now a newscaster for BBC television, based in London.

JOIN DREAMS COME TRUE!

Dreams Come True has become an important and successful charity due to the compassion and generosity of people such as yourself, donating money to enable the dreams of sick children to become a reality. In the six years of the charity so far more than 1,000 dreams have been fulfilled; but there are thousands more still to do.

It is essential that Dreams Come True has enough cash to continue with its crucial work. You can help by becoming a member of the charity. One year's membership costs £5 (£2 if you are under 18), and for this you will receive a membership badge as well as newsletters packed with stories of the charity's activities and what the stars have been doing to help, plus brilliant fund-raising ideas.

Please send your name, address and telephone number, together with a cheque or postal order to:

Dreams Come True
c/o Sheridans Solicitors
14 Red Lion Square
London WC1R 4QL

Every new member means a poorly child's dream will soon come true. Thank you.